French In

# Lower

# Normandy

## George East

French Impressions: Lower Normandy

Published by La Puce Publications

website: www.george-east.net

This paperback ISBN: 9781908747358

Typesetting and design by Francesca Brooks

e-pub: 9781908747372

mobi-kindle: 9781908747365

## About the Author

Once upon a time, George and Donella East moved to a ruined water mill on ten acres of rivers, woods, meadows and mud in Normandy. They intended living off the land and their wits, but literary fame and fortune intervened when George wrote a best-selling series of books about living with the enemy.

The couple then left the Mill of the Flea and moved on to an allegedly haunted manor-house on the vast Lower Normandy marshlands. Their next home was a rambling farmhouse half way up what counts as a mountain in Brittany. Then it was off to a remote hamlet in the Loire Valley.

Since then, the Easts have lived, tarried in or at least travelled slowly through every one of France's 13 regions and 90-odd mainland departments. This is the sixth in the French Impressions series, and George means to continue his sometimes unsteady progress around the country until he runs out of breath - or of friends and readers prepared to give him house room.

## Author's Note

The clue to what the reader will find in this book comes with the name of the series. This is certainly not a travel guide filled with factual information; rather the pages are daubed with often hasty and sometimes inaccurate impressions of the places and people encountered while travelling several thousand miles around Lower Normandy. As fans of the 19th-century art movement will tell you, an impression can sometimes give a truer picture than a carefully detailed and studied work.

Sometimes, of course, it can also end up as a bit of a dog's breakfast.

Thanks and apologies where necessary are due to everyone who helped with the latest *Impressions*. Special thanks are due to the Normandy Tourist Board and Brittany Ferries for their help during the research stages. They did not ask for any credit or credits, so my thanks are sincere.

Caen
O

CALVADOS (14)

ORNE (61)

Alençon
O

Saint-Lo
O

MANCHE
(50)

Cherbourg

# Like Southern England. Not.

Normandy gets its name from the Viking 'Northmen' who regularly raped and pillaged and finally settled in this part of France in the 9th Century so they would not have so far to travel to work.

From those chaotic beginnings came the establishment of the Duchy of Normandy, and we all know what happened in 1066 when William the Conqueror came calling. Because of this, the English have much in common in terms of language and culture with the people of Normandy, though our Continental cousins might not agree.

Taking up an area the size of the whole of south-eastern England, Normandy is home to around three million people and even more cows.

Like the other twelve regions, Normandy is divided into geographical *départéments* or, as you and I might say, counties. Unlike most of the other regions, Normandy is a place of two halves. Or it is according to the people who live there. Once upon a time, Metropolitan (mainland) France was divided into 22 regions. To save money and bureaucratic overkill, that number was reduced to thirteen on the 1st of January 2016. Those may be the clinical facts, but the demarcation and difference still lives on in the hearts of most Normans.

Although it is not why they were so named, there is a general feeling that Upper Normandy is a bit swankier than Lower Normandy.

*Haute-Normandie* is closer to Paris, has lots of posh resorts, grand racehorse studs and Claude Monet's famous gardens. *Basse-Normandie* has the D-Day beaches, all those *cows, some wonderful cheese and seafood - and is the birthplace of William the Conqueror.

There are three departments in Lower Normandy, namely Manche, Calvados and Orne. Each has its own identity, traditions, favourite food and drink and even ways of thinking. Obviously they share a similar climate, but even that can vary.

Generally speaking, the climate in Northern France can be

likened to Southern England. But as in other matters and even though divided only by the English Channel (or, as the French like to call it, *La Manche)*, Southern England and Normandy might as well be oceans apart.

As in England, it rains not infrequently and the weather can be changeable on a daily or hourly basis. There is an old saying in Normandy that all four seasons may be seen in one day. While I have not seen snow in August, the weather certainly can be erratic. Of course, the rain is why the place is so green and produces such good grass and so many contented cows - and cheeses to die for. Given their usual fat content, this is not such an inappropriate expression.

The landscape varies markedly within the three departments. The coastline of La Manche and parts of Calvados is generally flat and sandy, which is what made it so suitable for the D-Day invasion. But there are also plenty of rugged cliffs both on the coast and inland. And before you question the idea of cliffs without sea, *falaise* is French for 'crags' as well as 'cliffs', and the town of that name is famed as the birthplace of William the Conqueror.

Towards the middle of the region there is an enchantingly undulating area known by the locals as the Norman Switzerland. Further south, the very agricultural Orne is landlocked and is the most modest of the departments in financial terms. These topographical and geographical factors naturally affected the development of activity and cuisine and tradition.

As to population, no more than a hundred people are to be found in every square kilometre of the region - if you can find them. This compares with a population density of nearly five times that in the county of Hampshire, which is just across the water. The stereotypical image of sleepy Norman villages deserted at mid-day with even some restaurants closed for lunch can actually be a true one.

Overall, Lower Normandy is as disparate from the rest of France as any other region. This diversity is what makes the country so fascinating to so many people from other lands. France tops the list of most-visited countries worldwide, and

Normandy is one of the most popular tourist regions. The Normans know just what a gem of a place they live in, and can be unusually (compared with some parts of France) welcoming to visitors.

Finally, lots of Brits who have visited Normandy say it is just like England must have been a hundred years ago. This is obviously not so, but when you go there, you can see what they mean...

*More than half of all dairy production in France takes place in Lower Normandy and its next-door neighbour, Brittany.*

The flag and coat of arms of this region is another reminder of the close connections between Normandy and England.

The familiar three lions passant guardent was adopted by the Plantagenets in the late 12th century, when Richard I used them to represent his triple titles of King of England, Duke of the Normans and Duke of the Aquitaines. Technically, the lions are or were leopards. At some time one of the Norman lions/leopards was removed, and the standard Upper and Lower Normandy flag now features two. Along the lines of the legend about the Tower of London being safe as long as ravens live there, there's a story of how the third leopard was stolen but the people knew that as long as there were two left they would be able to breed, and Normandy would never cease to exist.

We are rolling down the link span and on to French soil, and I lower a window and take a deep breath of the rich sea air, salted with the heady bouquet of coffee, freshly baked croissants and stale tobacco.

Even after all these years I still feel a frisson of excitement and anticipation when arriving in France. I am often asked why I so like being here and travel about so much. The short answer is, like many travel writers, I always want to be where I am not, and France has become my favourite place to be a generally welcome stranger and traveller.

The crossing from Portsmouth was smooth and the book-signing a modest success. The kiosk sold out of my latest book, and it is always good to meet readers and learn of their thoughts on France. Of those kind enough to buy one of my books, some were on special-offer breaks, some visiting friends or relatives who lived in France, and more than a few had plans to become expatriates. Most would be retiring, but some would need to make a living out of living in France. Thankfully, none had plans to open a restaurant and show the French a thing or two about classy cooking.

I was also approached by a curious child who asked if I was Crimbo the Clown, and an elderly lady asked if I had been ill. When I asked why, she said I looked a lot older than the photograph on the cover of my new book.

Overall, I think our first on-board book signing was a success and proved a diversion for the older passengers. As it is high summer and most of the thousand or so passengers were under 12, Pirate Pete, Marvo the Magician and the Disco Dancing Competition proved far more of an attraction than the Famous Author.

But now we are free and the fairly open road and any number of as-yet unknown small adventures lie ahead. Though we have planned the journey in detail, it is a truism of all travel that though you may know where you are going, you cannot know what will happen on the way.

# CAEN

If I were a writer of that sort of travel guide, I would without hesitation award five stars to the capital of Lower Normandy.

The parameters for my assessment of any town we stay in or pass through include size, location, history, aesthetic appeal and that elusive but tangible air and quality which can truly be described as *je ne sais quoi.*

Although size should not matter, we find many small towns have too much of the bad bits like traffic and noise, but lack the interest of somewhere big enough to have a lively buzz and a good bit of history. With a population of more than a hundred thousand, Caen is well down the list of big French towns, but is nicely alive without being manic.

As to location and setting, the town is surrounded by the rich and rolling countryside of Calvados and yet less than ten miles from the sea. It is connected to the port of Ouistreham by road, river, canal and a superbly maintained bicycle path. This path continues due south to the heart of the glorious Suisse Normande, but more of that anon. It may be coincidental, but of all French towns we know, Caen is the most cycle-friendly.

It is also a town of deep contrasts, with the outskirts as ugly and off-putting as the centre is appealing. This is because most of Caen was leveled by the Allies after the D-Day landings and is ringed by a forest of post-war concrete apartment blocks. At its heart, though, there is treasure to be found.

Yet another place with a claim to an Arthurian connection Caen is said to have been named by King Arthur for Sir Kay. Historically, it is most associated with William the Conqueror. The town was key to his ambitions, and it was here he built what was to be one of Europe's largest fortified medieval castles. It is also where he was buried in 1087.

As a proper travel guide author would likely say, Lower Normandy's leading town has a long and turbulent history. The Battle of Caen in 1346 came at the start of the Hundred Years' War when Edward III took the town in one day. Spool on nearly six centuries and it was the Allies turn. They killed fewer citizens than Edward but did far more damage, destroying 70 percent of the town. But some fine buildings survived, often looking distinctly out of place amongst the plain, post-war designs.

Perfectly exemplifying this contrast, Caen boasts one of the most ornate and over-the-top town halls in France. Other places to visit include the emotion-evoking Memorial for Peace, and a brace of abbeys. As their names make clear (although it is a normal arrangement with these sort of buildings), one is for men and the other for women. They were built by William to gain absolution from the Pope for marrying his cousin.

Near the castle there's an attractive inland port and you can get around cheaply by a complex network of what Caennais call guided buses, and what you and I might call trams. Their routes are sacrosanct, and pedestrians and cyclists venture on or near the tracks at their peril. Elsewhere on road and even pavement the bicycle is treated almost with reverence, which is another reason we find Caen our sort of town.

~

We have found the Fountain Hotel, but not without some little travail and much travel.

In our experience, a hotel which is hard to find can be a good or bad thing. Either it is tucked away nicely in a side street, or many a mile from the interesting bits of a town. Worse, it might not exist at all. We booked the Hôtel de la Fontaine on-line, and in spite of the map have spent half an hour going the wrong way down one-way roads and enraging the drivers of guided buses and other road users. We have circled the castle at least a dozen times, and even been flagged down by tourists thinking our bright blue little Citroen is doing guided tours.

After joining a queue for the slipway at the inland port and almost joining the lines of expensive yachts floating in the marina, I saw two burly members of the *Gendarmerie* loitering on a corner. Approaching from behind, I addressed them in oily tones as 'Sirs', then realised my mistake when the biggest and broadest turned to face me. She had a faint seven o' clock shadow and an impressive scar down one cheek but the bow-front of her protective jacket confirmed her female gender. Fortunately she took my error in good part and even looked faintly pleased that I had mistaken her for a bloke.

When I asked if they knew the Fountain Hotel and where it was they both looked as if I had asked them if they knew of a short cut to the Hindu Kush. Following the classic Gallic shrug that can mean anything from 'Am I bothered?' to 'Why would you want to go to a dump like that?' the female officer takes a deep breath and launches in to a verbal and physical set of instructions. Seeing my eyes glaze over, she is kind enough to tear a page from her notebook and draw a diagram that looks slightly less complex than the escape route from Hampton Court Maze.

Half an hour later and two more visits to the marina and three turns around the castle and we have found the Hôtel de la Fontaine. Its hard-to-find-ness is actually a very good thing, as it stands in a narrow one-way street behind a huge department store and is literally not much more than a couple of stone's throws from the castle. We must have driven within a very short stone's throw at least a dozen times. It looks as if the road is little used and, even better, there is a parking space right outside. I see that a bar takes up the whole ground floor of the hotel, which can also be a good or bad thing. Some of our most enjoyable overnights have been spent in rooms above bars, but also some of our worst. Whether this one will suit us will depend on what sort of clientele patronise the establishment, what time it shuts, the general *ambience*, amiability of the staff and the price of refreshments.

Outside the bar, the pavement is taken up with a raised wooden terrace, which can be another good or bad thing. As we unload the Picasso, I notice the expensive 4x4 we have parked next to was registered in Russia. Beyond it are vehicles from Italy, Romania and Germany, so it appears the Hôtel de la Fontaine has an international clientele.

Through the tall doors is a pleasantly distressed vestibule, furnished with a pot plant and a notice advising guests that Reception is to be found on the first floor. On the way up I take hold of a rail screwed loosely to the wall, and arrive at the office still carrying it.

The owner seems unperturbed and reassures me that the rail comes away from its seating frequently. She props it in the corner and says cheerfully that her husband will see to it when he returns from Morocco.

Alexandra is a young, slim and attractive woman with all the qualifications for running a budget hotel. She is clearly tolerant and probably unshockable, and any rules and regulations will probably be applied as loosely as the hand rail in the corner. More indications that this is our sort of hotel when, before showing us to our room she takes us to her private kitchen and shows us how to work the kettle and microwave and stove. She even invites us to use the fridge or freezer, and help ourselves to bread if we run out when the shops are closed.

The room we are allotted has everything we need. It is clean, with a big bed, a cupboard or two and even a shower and toilet. This is a bonus as many budget hotels have a shared bathroom on each floor, which surprises and sometimes shocks younger more fastidious travellers who do not know that was once the norm.

As we return to the office to pick up a guide to the fleshpots, we are joined by a big dog. Alex obviously dotes on him, and tells us his name is *Joie*. She inherited him from an English guest and he was originally called Joe, but the proprietor of the Fountain Hotel renamed him because he had given her and her husband so much joy.

~

To the visitor it would seem that the relevant authorities have imposed an early evening curfew on anyone over 30.

We are sitting outside a bar near the grandiose Hotel de Ville and watching the world go by. It is a very young world. The median age seems around 22, and it looks as if there is also a ban on ugly people taking to the streets.

Like Brittany Ferries' Clara, the girls all seem effortlessly stylish as they stroll, stride or sashay past. You will find attractive and stylish young women in any large town in France or anywhere else, but these Caennaise are something special. The most noticeable thing is that though they are uniformly attractive, nearly all differ in their chosen style of presentation. Some opt for summery dresses and sandals, some for thick tights and high heels. One girl manages to make a camouflage top and trousers and a calf-high pair of paratroopers' boots look sexy.

It is noticeable that the tables around us are almost exclusively occupied by young men. It is obviously their job to sit and watch the parade. Seated and mostly immobile, the only way they can draw attention to themselves is by the way they smoke and drink. A tall, slim boy who looks barely old enough to drink even in France is pretending not to notice the river of passing pulchritude, and is in animated conversation with another even slimmer youth at the next table. His arms flap and gyrate like those of a marionette with an unskilled operator, and he occasionally punctuates his remarks with stabs of his cigarette before returning it to hang precariously from his upper lip.

Then we notice something else different about the constant stream of young women parading by. There is not a single tattoo on display, nor a single wobble. There are no illustrated women, and certainly no fat ones. As my wife also points out, none of the dozens of slim young women and girls have been competing to show off their midriffs. Were we in our home town of Portsmouth on a fine summer Saturday evening, dozens of young women would have been displaying their belly-button piercings and the hearts, stars, songbirds or even lines from poems they will never read indelibly inscribed on their bodies. Many would look as if they were wearing a sizeable lifebelt of flesh. Perhaps the fashion will spread to provincial France, but looking at the beautiful and slim young women of Caen it is hopefully a long way off.

~

We have moved on and are taking our ease outside a *bar-tabac* on the busy road passing the castle. It is noisy and cold but there are more customers outside than in. Even in chillier regions, the French like to sit outside bars and restaurants so they can enjoy watching what is going on while they eat and drink.

A middle-aged, oppressed-looking woman is sitting at the next table, but she is too occupied to take much notice of the passing tide of people and traffic. In a somehow French way she is managing to drink, smoke and scrape away at her trio of scratch cards at the same time. As each one fails to reveal a win, she shrugs her acceptance, takes a sip of wine and a drag on her cigarette and moves on to the next card. She meets my eye, smiles and gives a pout and a shrug. She is clearly communicating that she knows she is wasting her time, but maybe, just maybe, her time will come. Then, the world had better watch out.

I especially like *bar-tabacs* when they have a PMU license which allows various forms of gambling to take place on the premises. As far as I know you cannot get a drink at most betting shops in Britain, and I suspect it would not work nearly as well as it does here. The clientele at the typical PMU is mostly male, and the average punter stands at the bar with his *demi* of beer flattening as he makes his selection for the day and watches the racing on the big screen.

Even when a PMU is near-empty there is usually an air of suppressed excitement and anticipation. I think this may be because, as the notices on the walls of past big wins prove, someone will strike it lucky sometime soon.

Rather than a race card, we are studying form on a map Alex gave us earlier. It is the official guide to places of interest in the city centre, to which she had added her own recommendations. She has heavily circled an area lying almost in the shadow of the castle, where there seems to be a street containing nothing but restaurants.

As the lady at the next table comes to the end of her scratching routine and reaches for her glass, I ask if she can recommend a good place to eat for little money in the immediate vicinity. This sets her off on a really extreme bout of shrugging and nodding, which I know means she believes she holds the key to our evening eating happiness. You have to remember that shrugs in France can signal much more than disinterest or fatalistic acceptance. I have actually seen long and obviously detailed conversations taking place without a single word being uttered.

Realising we are foreigners, the lady speaks with her voice as well as her shoulders, and says without question we must go to a little family-run bistro at the top of the street alongside the castle. It specialises in regional cuisine, and we will be able to eat and drink ourselves around France for less than fifty Euros.

As I thank her and start to fold the map, a loud tutting noise emanates from another table. At it stands the waiter who served us earlier. He is giving the Gallic shrug which I know signifies a minor rebuke. The customer is not always right, it appears, as he tells us there is a much better and cheaper and closer restaurant.

From within the PMU comes a mixture of groans, grunts and sighs indicating approval or disagreement, and I realise I have committed a cardinal error. To ask in a busy bar in France for advice on the best place to eat is like asking the individual members of a particularly rabid fan club who they think is the cutest member of One Direction.

~

At this time, Caen's road of restaurants reminds me of Regent Street on the first day of the January sales. There must be two dozen establishments competing for attention, and they all seem to be under siege.

Although it is much too early to eat, hundreds of people are patrolling the cobbled passageway. Unlike combatants at the January sales, they are not looking for a bargain; in fact, price will be a minor consideration as they decide what and where to eat. Some couples and groups look as if they have been at it for hours, and mild disagreements are threatening to turn into public rows. As demonstrated by the near-fracas in the PMU, the French can be very fussy when it comes to food and the best place to eat it apart from their homes. Especially on a sacred weekend dining-out night.

We join the throng, and I cannot but notice that we, or rather I, am getting some curious glances. My wife points out that nearly everyone is decked out in their Saturday-evening-eating-out finery. Even she has put a dress on, but I had refused to change from what she calls my stand-alone shorts. This is the sobriquet she has given my favourite cycling trousers, and the name is because she believes that if I were to step out of them they would remain stolidly upright. She also believes I and they have become so attached over the years that they would follow me like a faithful dog if I left home without them.

It is true they have weathered many a storm and absorbed a great deal of chain oil, spilled drink and food debris over the years, but this has helped make them waterproof and even more durable. In fact they are so rigid I believe I could use them as a sail and travel at a comfortable rate with the wind behind and my legs akimbo and absolutely no need to pedal. In short, they have become a comfortable as well as practical travelling companion.

But however suitable they are for riding, they do not seem to be *à la mode* for dining out in style. As well as curious looks from the crowd, I note I am getting haughty looks from some of the waiters and touts standing at the entrance to the more up market establishments.

It is in fact interesting to see the different approach from these guardians at the gates. Those outside the obviously popular and most expensive restaurants look as if they will insist on references and a credit check before allowing customers in. Others trying to drum up business outside less popular venues simper and try to look seductive and winsome, a bit like a working girl at King's Cross on a slow night. I can see their problem, as there is certainly a lot of competition on hand.

Each side of the winding cobbled street is lined with places which are as distinctively different in appearance as the cuisine they offer. A twee thatched cottage poses as an English hostelry complete with rustic seating, fake barrels and swing sign and promises a bill of fare I bet was never on the menu at a typical country pub in the Middle Ages.

Next door is a minimalist trattoria, all black marble and plate glass and stereotypical Italian waiters. Beyond that, a Japanese sushi house competes for attention with a classical French establishment which looks as elegant and probably as pricey as any to be found in the hotspots of Paris.

We reach the end of the road and return as waiters and touts avoid eye contact. Gradually, the crowd thins as groups decide on which establishment to patronise. Eventually, we find ourselves in a strange rag-tag group for some reason composed of a mix of very fat and very thin people. They are heading down a side street, and we are drawn along with them like flotsam on a fast-flowing tide.

~

We have been shown to a table on the terrace of the restaurant where we were washed ashore. We were lucky to get a seat, not just because of the number of would-be customers but the sheer size of some of them. We are hemmed in by probably the total complement of obese individuals in Caen. There are plenty of fat people in France of course, but it is curious to see so many assembled under one roof. In strict contrast and dotted amongst the fatties are tables of thin, young people. I suggest they might be emergency rations if the gargantuan diners get peckish, but my wife says it is obvious they are students. Students. All students are always hungry, and these have obviously come to eat their weight in an effort to sustain them through the week. The reason they and their meaty fellow diners have come here is because it is a *buffet-volonté* restaurant.

As *buffet* is French for 'sideboard', and *volonté* means 'at will', the expression means you can eat as much as you like for a set price. If you have ever wondered why we refer to some help-yourself events as 'flying buffets', the simple explanation is probably a misinterpretation.

The idea of paying a set price and then pigging out is of course very popular in Britain, particularly in Chinese and Indian outlets. I have eaten at dozens of such establishments in

France, and if anything, customers seem to take and eat less than they would if their meal were served to them.

This is clearly not the case here. A huge board outside the entrance invites diners to help themselves to a variety of meats and vegetable, and then to cook what they choose. I have never seen the appeal of paying to do a cook's job, but is obviously a popular concept here. There is also unlimited access to soft drinks and wine, with a cautionary note above the tap in the fake barrel reminding the patrons to drink sensibly.

There is no such caution with regard to the food, and some customers are clearly having a problem getting their hugely over-laden plates back to their tables. Some resourceful diners have lightened the load by grazing off the plates as they go.

Eventually, a waiter arrives at our table to explain he is not a waiter. He goes through the routine with a series of suitable hand signals like an air steward giving the pre-flight address. First, we should make our choice from the dozens of sliced vegetables and present our plate to the vegetable chef. Then, while they were being cooked over a fire, we should choose from the meat counter. Having selected steak, sausage, offal or all three, we would need to put them in the holder provided and cook them to our satisfaction over the charcoal grill. Again like a flight attendant, he produces a strange device which looks like an implement found in a well-equipped medieval torture chamber. It is an ovoid metal cage about a foot long, with a handle at one end. It seems the idea is to put your meats into the cage, adding raw peppers or other veggie bits to make a shish kebab without the shish. He offers to demonstrate but I say I will pick it up as we go along, grab two of the mini-iron maidens and make for the fire.

~

Lord Byron said that for all its volumes, history only has one page. I think he meant that we do not learn from the past and keep on making the same mistakes, and my wife says this is certainly true of me.

She is tucking in to a plateful of succulent gobbets of bloody beef. Alongside is a side plate bearing a trio of XXL-size Breton sausages, and her concession to a balanced meal is a single mushroom. I am watching her eat with the lust of a man who sees something he usually craves, but is unable to manage.

My mistake was being too impatient to wait for the meat to cook, and spoiling the meal by my excesses. The dozens of vegetables on offer are all sliced thinly, so they are easy to eat but just as difficult to digest. Along with the four bowls of julienned tomato, onion, white and red cabbage, yellow and green peppers, cauliflower and aubergine, I helped myself to seven slices of poppy seed bread and five glasses of wine from the tap in the wall. Now I can only sit and groan and watch as my wife deliberately smacks her lips with pleasure over the contents of our iron maidens.

Other diners have more staying power and capacity than me. A very large woman on the next table is making her way back from her third visit to the grill area. Her small and slight husband finished eating some time ago, but for propriety's sake she takes two plates at a time and pretends one is for him. Across from us, five studenty types are vying to see who can drink and eat the most in the shortest time. Next to them, a fastidious-looking man with a German accent and what appears to be a naturally disapproving air summons the flight attendant to point out that his cage has several small lumps of cooked meat adhering to it, obviously from previous usage. With a magnificent unconcern, the attendant said that the bits were deliberately left in place as they enhanced the flavour during the cooking process.

~

My wife has at last finished her meal and is helping me towards the door. In passing I ask the flight attendant if the establishment could provide me with a doggie bag. He raises an eyebrow and explains that the establishment is not a takeaway, even if we had a dog.

~

Midnight has come and gone, but we are loath to go to the hotel and abandon the streets. I also need a good walk to try and digest the results of my vegetable orgy.

It is a balmy night, the air relieved by a light breeze. The moon is waxing gibbous, and the neon glare from the man-made canyons lined with giant department stores makes our passage lighter than day. Our footsteps are our only companions, the town centre is completely deserted, and it is as if we own Caen.

There is an elegant park behind the hotel, and it is obviously home to a huge colony of starlings and a handful of *clochards*, or as we used to say, tramps. As we left the hotel earlier, we heard and saw the starlings descend on the row of plane trees, and I lost count at 347. The handful of human occupants are obviously seasoned rough sleepers as they are scorning the local *foyer* where they could get a free meal and comfortable bed for the night. Contrary to most people's perception, it is an undeniable truth that some homeless people choose to live on the streets.

The group on the bench next to ours is gathered around a demijohn of something red, which they pass from hand-to-hand, watching intently as each one takes a draught to see that he or she is not taking more than a reasonable swallow. They talk animatedly, and hand-rolled cigarettes and dog-ends are flourished to punctuate the conversation. A friendly and apparently self-reliant gathering, they have asked us for nothing and already offered us a swig from the jar.

The party grows louder and other members of the open-air community are arriving for a nightcap. One man shuffles towards us and he could be anywhere from middle age to elderly. His beard and hair are long and his face beaten by weather and drink and falls or attacks. He is wearing the remains of a dark suit, the bottoms of the trousers frayed almost theatrically. Incongruously, his feet are clad in what looks like a new pair of elaborately carved clogs. He moves slowly but with a certain dignity, graciously accepting a few Euros from me as he passes and making no attempt to hide his windfall from his comrades.

As he shares out the money, I am struck by the similarities and the contrasts with the diners in the street of restaurants. The main difference is that many of the people eating at the restaurants will be rich almost beyond compare with the members of this gathering. The diners did not seem any happier than these casualties of life, and I wonder how fate or circumstance dictates who ends up where. Some would say success and failure are the result of ambition and application with luck playing no part, but I think that is too easy an answer. The *clochards* may have lost out in the race for status and wealth, but however much most of the people in the street of restaurants laughed and smiled, they did not seem particularly happy to have won it.

# Pegasus Bridge

A few minutes after midnight on the 6th of June 1944, a force of 181 men landed by glider close to where we are now standing. They were led by Major John Howard, and their mission was to take a bridge spanning the Caen canal.

The bridge was won after a brief firefight, but not without loss. Lance Corporal Fred Greenhalgh drowned in a pond when his glider landed, and Lieutenant Den Brotheridge was killed when crossing the bridge. He was the first Allied serviceman to be killed by enemy fire during the D-Day invasion.

Renamed for the shoulder flash worn by the British troops and replaced in 1994, *Pegasus Bridge serves several functions. It is a monument and tourist attraction, and is also a working, moving bridge which makes an impressive spectacle when in action. We are on the ten-mile ride on the towpath midway between Caen and the port of Ouistreham, and have arrived just in time to see the show.

Gears grind, making a groaning sound like a giant with stomach cramps, lights flash and sirens sound, cameras flash and people point and children shout with excitement as the whole section spanning the river starts to rise.

The reason for the bridge swinging into action is a disappointingly small yacht which is chugging along the canal from the direction of the marina at Ouistreham. The bridge appears unmanned and must be operated from elsewhere, but it seems a lot of trouble to go to just to let one small boat through.

It is a busy road and regular users must be caught frequently, but this is one of the few times I have seen the French seemingly happy to wait in line. Or if not happy, resigned and untroubled. Some of the drivers who have obviously seen it all before leave their vehicles and stretch their legs, have a cigarette or a chat, and I notice one truck driver hurries into the nearby cafe. There are no toilets inside, so he is probably aiming to snatch a quick coffee or something stronger.

The queue of traffic grows and there are more ooohs and

aahs as several tons of tarmac and metal reach for the sky.

In the canal, the yacht is slowing down although it is still some distance from the bridge. It looks even smaller now, and there is enough leeway for a boat three times its size to pass under the raised link span.

Then there is an alarmed murmur from the crowd and I see the prow of the yacht is turning towards the towpath. It bumps into the grassy bank, and the man at the wheel calmly puts the engine into reverse. The moving part of the bridge has reached its zenith and there is an almost stunned silence as the yacht performs a clumsy three-point turn and starts to chug back towards Ouistreham. The skipper does not look back, and I am not surprised as there is an air of almost outraged disappointment hanging over the spectators.

After a while the giant gears grind and the link span starts to descend and we join the race to find a seat outside the famous café and discuss the drama. We will never know if the man at the wheel had just remembered he had a pressing engagement elsewhere or had never intended passing under the bridge and was, as we like to say in Portsmouth, having a laugh.

*The original bridge was replaced in 1994 and left to rot on a piece of waste ground until it was sold to the Pegasus Museum for the symbolic price of one franc. Many of the soldiers killed in local action during the Invasion are buried nearby at Ranville cemetery. Lt Brotheridge's resting place is to be found in the churchyard next to the cemetery.*

~

The Pegasus Bridge Café is said by some to be the first French home to be liberated after the D-Day landings. Astonishingly, it is still in the hands of Madame Arlette Gondrée, who was living there as a small child when the British troops arrived. It is not widely known that Arlette's mother and father were active in helping with the operation, which was codenamed *Coup de Main*.

Born and raised in Alsace, Thérèse Gondrée spoke fluent

German and would eavesdrop on soldiers before passing any useful information to the Resistance. It was she who was able to reveal the exact location of the trigger mechanism intended to set off the explosives wired to the bridge in the case of an attack, and of Rommel's plans for an anti-tank gun emplacement to be placed by the bridge.

Immediately after the engagement the cafe was designated as 7th Battalion's HQ and Regimental Aid post. To celebrate the success of the operation, Georges Gondrée dug up nearly a hundred bottles of Champagne he had buried in the back garden at the start of the Occupation. He offered free drinks to all, and Major Howard responded by ordering all his men to report sick to the new Aid post so they could share in the celebrations. The tradition continues to this day, and no member of the 6th Airborne Division has ever had to pay for a drink at the Cafe Gondrée.

Together with it being in the same hands, the most satisfying aspect of the Pegasus Cafe for us was how un-commercial and apparently unchanged was the building and its interior. Somehow and in spite of the cars and coaches and throng of tourists, it looks and feels exactly like the rural French bars I remember as a child. The interior is cool and dark and there are no modern furnishings or equipment, and the open door to the living quarters could have been a time portal. Framed in the doorway was the huge table covered in patterned oilskin, with a centrepiece of a vase containing flowers. Beyond that, the monumental buffet displaying the family's best china. Even the wallpaper seemed of the period. Perhaps if I stood there long enough I would see into the past as Thérèse Gondrée laid the table as her husband opened a bottle of good wine. As the elderly lady who took my money, thanked me and moved towards the doorway, I somehow expected her to step through it and become again the little girl who welcomed her brave liberators.

# Ouistreham

I like Ouistreham.

There is something about ports, and especially cross-Channel ports, which appeals to me. It may be that there is something going on at the docks 24/7, or simply that a port is a means of escape as well as a place of arrival.

Pleasingly for me, Ouistreham is not much more than a point of arrival and departure for the ferry companies, and the town seems to exist only to serve the port. There are hardly any outskirts, and no surrounding sprawl of commercial activity or skyscrapers of containers.

You simply roll off the ferry and through the checkpoint and you are in Ouistreham and France. It is almost as if, like villages grew around castles to serve the needs of those inside, Ouistreham grew or adapted to look after people using the port. Consequently, there are dozens of hotels, restaurants, bars and tobacco outlets clustered around the port area. All are vying for custom, and the competition means you can usually get a good deal. Interestingly and perhaps surprisingly, there are no Chinese or Indian eating places to attract the millions of Britons passing through every year. But there are some very good traditional French-style outlets, or you can get something with chips at almost any time. Perhaps the local businesses are so good at what they do because they have been at it so long. Although it looks modern as the inevitable result of the D-Day Landings, Ouistreham has been a trading post since the Middle Ages. The name comes from the old French for oyster (ouistre) and the Saxon term for a small dwelling, 'ham'.

It was from here that the Allies fought their way to Pegasus Bridge, the honour of leading the assault being given to Free French Commando.

Whenever we are passing through, we leave plenty of time to take a spin on the bikes, and Ouistreham is, like Caen, sternly cycle-friendly. From the ferry port due south, there is the beautifully-maintained cycle route to Caen alongside the waterway and past Pegasus Bridge.

Westward from the port entrance there's a very long and continuous promenade with a dedicated cycle way travelling past the Bella Riva beaches and a host of small touristy villages. The other way, there's a bridge over the canal which takes you on a short ride eastwards past what looks almost like a shanty town of huts and cabins, some of which have grown to become full-time homes. The scene reminds me of my childhood in Portsmouth when the same thing was allowed to happen and before the houseboats and shacks were swept brutally away to make room for civilisation. From the ever-deserted beach here you can watch the giant ferries dock and depart, fishing boats come and go and seabirds go about their business. When we cease our endless travels through France, this apparently neglected corner within easy cycle range of a big, sophisticated city would be a very nice place to come to rest.

Suiting its status as the head town of the region, Caen has two significant waterways.

One is the canal which connects the town centre with the port of Ouistreham. The other waterway is the River Orne, which runs alongside the canal. The river sources in the department named for it, and on its journey to the sea feeds the canal.

Opened in 1857, the canal was a relatively modest channel with a depth of no more than four metres. Now it is a much grander affair, with two locks and a number of quays. Incoming goods include exotic woods, and exports include cereals from the vast fields surrounding the town.

The Orne passes through Caen, and the canal starts in the heart of the town at the basin of St Pierre. Nowadays it serves as a marina for risibly expensive yachts rather than working barges, and each week it is the venue for what must be one of the biggest and busiest markets in all Normandy. Caen has a market for every day of the week, but the Sunday *Marché Saint Pierre* is the daddy of them all.

~

Acres of colourful awnings, stalls and vans surround the inland port, and it is as if a great caravan has stopped off at an oasis. There are no camels in evidence, but the alleyways between the stalls are already clogged with people. Back from our spin along the canal towpath, we lock up our bikes and join the throng.

Contra-intuitively, as sociologists like to say, I have always found the French at their most polite and considerate at big and busy events. In an everyday situation, they will abandon their cars like the British leave litter and I have even seen drivers block off a road completely if it gets them a little nearer to their objective. Yet at any large countryside show they will meekly park in the exact spot in a field to which they are directed. In a busy outdoor market like this they jink and swerve adroitly and collisions and confrontations and altercations are rare.

Perhaps the French have a more acute sense of self-preservation, or are more naturally balletic. People of all ages and both genders seem to relish confrontation at British boot sales, and I have the scars to prove it.

We follow our noses and enter a long and odiferous passage of vans and stalls offering fresh bread, vegetables, fish, meat, cheese and Italian, Spanish, Vietnamese, Moroccan, and other African delicacies. We pass a stall with dozens of open containers of spices and herbs on show and the mélange of odours becomes almost intoxicating.

Suddenly, the bouquet is replaced with the sharp tang of tanned hide, and we find ourselves in a land of giants. The stallholders in this section are probably Sudanese or Somali, and all tower above the tallest of the passers-by. Astonishingly, the *average* height in the Sudan is 6ft 4 inches for men, and six feet for women. Hussain Bisad is a Somali and currently the tallest man in the world at nearly 7ft 8 inches. He weighs 210 kilograms (just over 33 stone) and his feet are size 26. The men selling bags, belts and other leather goods here are below seven feet, but not by much.

One magnificent figure in a long black robe and skin like polished ebony is on eye level with me, but he is sitting on a stool with his knees up to his chin. He is casually beating out a complex rhythm on a set of bongo drums with fingers almost the size and length of standard drum sticks. When he sees my admiring look he smiles and invites me to have ago. I see that the stall behind him is lined with all sorts of African drums with expensive price tags, so politely decline. Although I would love to hear his sales pitch, my wife gave me a formal warning before we arrived and I understand her concern. I have a weakness for buying things simply because they seem a bargain, especially at this sort of event.

We let the crowd carry us on and turn into a row where there is enough sugar on sale to keep all the dentists in the town in lucrative employment for life.

For a race so creative when it comes to cooking, the French seem surprisingly unimaginative when it comes to types and flavours of sweets. In England you can still get sherbet-filled Flying Saucers, aniseed balls and monkey nuts; here the main constituents seem to be dye and sugar in various shapes.

Next we pass through corridors of shoes and handbags and hats and coats and tops and skirts and dresses and trousers. As usual, nearly all the stalls are aimed at female customers, and as usual the garments show that not all French women go for elegant understatements in fashion terms.

From be-spangled denim trousers and crochet tops decorated with multi-coloured ribbons, we arrive at the end of the market proper and the start of a section where I am at my happiest but in most danger. My wife confiscates all the notes and loose change I have in my pocket, and I am free to enter a world of fascination.

I once staged a boot sale in the fields of our mill in Normandy, and several people who had seen the posters came along with old boots to sell. In France, they call the disposal of unwanted household goods a *vide grenier*, or empty loft. A larger, regular market might be called a *marché aux puces*, or flea market, or a *brocante*.

This is the point at which my wife always issues the final warning about buying things we do not need based on price. I appreciate her concern and am still trying to get rid of a leather-bound Complete Works of Shakespeare I bought recently at a boot sale in Brittany. I got the item for a snip, but there seems little interest on e-bay for the full range of the Bard's work in Breton.

The thing I find most fascinating about flea markets is that you could not invent the sort of things on sale that someone must have once found useful or collectable. On the first stall alone is a cornucopia of unwanted items, including a Satellite dish-style electric heater with bare wires protruding from the back, a very big game of Ludo played with plastic horses instead of counters, an art deco ashtray, a wig in the form of a Rastafarian's dreadlocks, and what looks like an original Conquistador's helmet. Alongside is a trader specialising in weaponry, and his offerings include machetes, butterfly and flick-knives, crossbows, samurai swords and what are hopefully imitation firearms and hand grenades. I am not tempted, as the price tags on the various weapons show how expensive it must be to be a Ninja warrior or mass murderer.

Next we pass a stall devoted to the taxidermist's art, and I struggle to avoid eye-contact with an understandably surprised-looking gazelle.

Reaching the quayside, we watch a group of young white people making a bad job of getting some trace of rhythm out of the sort of drums on sale at the giant Somali's stall. They look very earnest and intent but simply cannot reproduce the sort of repetitive, hypnotic thudding coming from the valley of the giants.

Back at our starting point, my wife unlocks her bike and sets off in high gear and dudgeon to the hotel, and I follow at a more measured rate. This is mainly because I am weighed down by a cast-iron marmite cooking pot I managed to sneak a bid in for while Donella was distracted. Our present home has no open fire, but I could not resist the price of just five Euros. Although unusable for its purpose, it will make an attractive garden planter and already has a built-in drainer in the shape of the hole in the bottom.

~

Our fears about the bar beneath our room were completely misplaced; it is not so much a bar as an up market grocery shop that sells drinks.

The idea of selling drinks with other goods or services is not uncommon in Normandy, as it was once so in Britain. Unusual locations I have taken a beer in include cake shops, a DIY establishment and even a camping supply store.

Once upon a time and before the supermarkets killed them off, every village in France would have its own *bar-epicerie*. Often run by a redoubtable and sometimes scary widow, there would be a small and usually eccentric selection of groceries one side of a bead curtain, and the bar on the other. Men were not encouraged to visit the grocery side, and the ladies of the village would choose not to patronise the bar. Sometimes apparently macho farm workers would be summoned from the bar by an unseen presence, and to hear was always to obey.

The bar beneath the Fountain Hotel is of the sort which could only survive in a place where people can afford to buy the very best or at least the most expensive grocery items.

The interior is all dark wood and cool marble and wrought iron. On the counter are artistic displays of the finest cheeses, and behind the servery hang rows of sausages and hams which would not deign to be seen in any supermarket. One wall is devoted to the display of vintage wines, and customers can sample them on the mezzanine floor. Unfortunately, as it is a Sunday the bar-cum-grocery store is closed and we are in search of a bar which is open. Although we are in the capital of Lower Normandy, most of the restaurants and apparently all the bars in the streets around the hotel are closed.

After walking at least a mile through the deserted canyons of the city centre we are about to give up when my wife spots a distant neon sign, blinking like a beacon in a lunar landscape.

We arrive to find it is a bar, and inside it is as if we have travelled in space and time and are somewhere in rural Brittany.

The familiar heavy wooden bar stools, benches and tables are completely out of keeping with the chromium plate and glass frontage. Posters on the wall show rugged coasts and landscapes and ladies in traditional costume with improbably high cylindrical *coiffes* (lace bonnets). The shelf behind the bar is stocked with Breton beers and ciders and the menu shows the chef's predilection for the butter and salt and buckwheat flour which dominates the Breton cuisine. At the bar are a couple of mature gentlemen who have obviously evaded the evening curfew on anyone even approaching middle age.

One is a small, wizened individual wearing hi-visibility overalls and gumboots and a visored safety helmet. Either he works at weekends or this is his idea of leisure wear. Delicately using a finger and thumb, the man lifts the visor to take a sip from his glass and I see he has a mischievous, rubicund, round and snub-nosed face. As Cornwall has its pixies, Brittany has its Korrigans, and this man could be a poster boy for the mischievous denizens of the hinterland of that region.

Next to him is a dignified figure dressed as if for an evening out in the 1930s. On his head is an obviously aged but immaculate homburg hat, and he is wearing an equally vintage dinner jacket with wide, shiny lapels. Around his shoulders is a white silk scarf, and a blood-red cravat blossoms from his open-necked shirt. Somewhat incongruously, he is wearing a pair of weathered trainers and his silver-topped cane leans against the bar. He nods graciously and lifts his glass in salute as the lady behind the bar bids us a good evening.

She is not dressed in Breton clothing, but to test my hunch I order our drinks and thank her in the language of that region. This is not to imply I can speak it, but while we lived there I soon learned some key words. They included 'hello', 'goodbye' 'a beer and a red wine, please', 'cheers' and 'the same again'.

The lady is obviously amused at my attempt, and after accepting a drink she explains that she is a former dancer from Rennes; she took the bar as an aid to her retirement some years ago. She likes to be an ambassador for her home region, thus the range of drinks and dishes - and the Sunday opening.

I notice as we talk that the man in the homburg hat scribbles on a beer mat and then passes it across the counter. The woman looks at it and smiles and says that he is complimenting me on my Breton. He is writing his remarks down not because he is shy, but because he cannot speak. He was a very talented saxophonist who played in the top venues of Rennes, but had to have his voice box removed to save his life when cancer came.

I nod and take the man's hand and ask if he will have a drink. He hesitates then writes on another beer mat and passes it over to the landlady. She says that he says he would much appreciate a glass of Breton apple brandy, but only if I will agree to have one with him in return. Then we must repeat the procedure with his friend. I should be warned that this could lead to an excess of drinking and eating and talking. This is, as I know, a very Breton approach to logic and consequence.

I look at my wife and smile and raise a finger for service. As I say to our new friend, it is a shame that we have found our sort of bar on our last night in Caen, but our visit could not have ended on a better note or in better company.

# Tripes à la mode de Caen

To add even more flavour to this book I asked my wife to look out some recipes linked with Lower Normandy.

As with our Bakewell tarts and Yorkshire puddings, every region of France will have at least one signature dish which is lauded by the others. Brittany has its crepes and galettes, Burgundy its Boeuf Bourguignon. Sometimes, quite a simple dish will be treated with what would seem to us to be undue reverence. Normandy, for instance, is famed for its rice pudding, which actually has its own Appreciation Society.

Nowadays on our side of the Channel, offal is far from popular, and tripe is generally regarded as, well, a load of tripe. Made of parts of the stomachs of various farm animals, tripe was a working-class staple or even a delicacy in Britain several generations ago. It is still highly thought of in France, and found in various guises on upmarket menus. *Tripes à la mode de Caen* is basically a stew made from beef offal, and said to have been invented by a monk at Caen abbey sometime during the middle Ages. Predictably, it is alleged to have been William the Conqueror's favourite dish. Just as predictably, it has its own fan club, loosely translated as The Golden Brotherhood of Tripe.

I have to confess that we have neither made nor eaten the stew served hot, but have bought and enjoyed it cold and solid (yes I know it sounds awful, but...) from specialist grocery shops when on a picnic.

If you want to have a go, here's how the Brotherhood recommends it be made:

Ingredients

1kg tripe
One calf's foot (for the gelatin)
200g bacon
400g onion
800g carrot
One bouquet garni
A clove
A glass of apple brandy (Calvados)
A glass of dry white wine
Seasoning

Method

Preheat the oven to $210^0$C.
Rinse the tripe and foot and cut them into fair-sized pieces.
Peel and chop the onions.
Cut the bacon into large pieces.
Peel and slice the carrots.
Place a layer of the onions into a suitable casserole dish, then a layer of bacon. Season.
Continue with a layer of tripe and calf's foot, then a layer of carrots, and repeat the sequence.
Finishing with a layer of tripe, pour over the brandy and wine, then add the herbs and spice and cook for at least six hours.

# ORNE

Green is certainly the colour of choice in this part of Lower Normandy.

The landscape is a gently undulating counterpane, divided into smallish fields of varying hue. Here and there are copses and woods made of deciduous trees, and the good, rich earth is laced with small streams.

Cows regard us incuriously as we pass, and sheep graze in small apple orchards. Now and then we pass a hamlet of cottages huddled round a church which would look at home anywhere in rural England. Occasionally we pass a village store and sometimes it will be open, but so far we have seen more animals than people. With less than fifty people occupying every square kilometre, the Orne is quiet even by French rural standards.

Once part of an ancient province, this is one of the 83 original *départements* formed during the French Revolution. No more than 30 miles from the coast, it is landlocked and surrounded by five other departments. It is not one of the wealthiest parts of northern France, and the population has actually declined to 300,000 since its high point in the mid 19th century.

Visitors from across the Channel would more than probably say how very much like the rural England of long ago it all looks, though I suspect the locals think it is quite French. But I know what the visitors mean. Increasingly, the British countryside has been riven with roads, and our villages become drive-through reminders of how things were. Across the country it has not been possible to escape the cost of so many people occupying such a small area. It does no good to complain about the inevitable, but here in this peaceful place is a poignant reminder of what we had and what we have lost.

# Pays d'Argentan

We have arrived at base camp.

Argentan sits comfortably on the river Orne and is the largest town in the north of the department. Like Caen and many other Norman towns it has a long and bloody history and has had a variety of owners and occupiers.

In its early days the Viking chief Rollo gifted it to one of his lieutenants, and throughout the Middle Ages it was either thriving or being razed to the ground, usually by attacking English forces. The town was badly damaged by bombing during the D-Day advances, and almost totally destroyed months later when the US Third Army under General George Patton took on and defeated two major *Panzer* tank divisions.

There is an ancient but much-abused and restored church in the centre of town and some interesting old buildings to investigate, but first we need to set up camp.

As usual, we shall be moving around the departments and stopping off at camp sites, friends' homes and, when there is no alternative, paid-for accommodation in hotels or B&Bs. As the years pass we find ourselves more and more drawn to sleeping under a proper roof and at least a foot above the ground, but the weather forecast is set fair so we will start with good intentions.

After checking out the alternatives, we have decided to spend a few days at the Municipal campsite. This is because it has good reviews, is within easy bike or walking distance of the centre yet away from noisy roads, and backs on to the river and miles of open countryside.

When we arrive, a small man with a big moustache appears to be hoovering the gravel fronting the office, which lies just beyond the barrier. We park at a discreet distance and watch as he lays down the vacuum cleaner and picks up a rake. With practiced ease, he moves backwards along the length of the driveway, swinging the rake in a precise arc like a man scything invisible grass. The result is a series of interlinking sworls in a pattern which was so popular on plastered ceilings and walls in

Britain forty years ago.

The problem comes when the driveway lives up to its name and a large car and caravan come scrunching up to stop at the office. The small man looks at the damage to his handiwork, sighs, lies down his rake and disappears through the door of the office. The driver of the tank-like German car follows him and we wait for sounds of a verbal or physical exchange.

There are none, so we park clear of the remains of the Artex design and enter the bureau. We wait while the German pays his bill and leaves to cause further damage to the warden's artwork.

While I show our credentials, Donella has a chat with the large parrot which appears to be in charge of the office. I learn later that his name is Joss and his English is better than mine. As well as his native French, he can swear and hold a limited conversation in German, Dutch and Italian.

Our human host introduces himself as Serge and, after going through the basic rules and requirements, leads us to the spare pitches. We pass a serried rank of gleaming camper and caravans, and Serge invites us to take our pick of the available spaces for tents. We choose a site with no neighbours and next to the hedge separating the campsite from the river bank. I say I will go and get the car and start unpacking, but Serge says I must wait until he has prepared the site. It looks perfectly okay to me, but I agree and watch as the warden fetches a serious-looking lawn mower and gives the patch of grass an even closer haircut.

Inviting us to drop in to the office if we want any advice on where to go and what to see in the town, Serge rumbles off. Before we start on unpacking the car I see that our warden has picked up his rake and is starting again on his Sisyphusian task.

~

Although it is clearly not as instantly and effortlessly erectable as advertised, Donella put our new tent up in less than five minutes, helped or (as she said) hindered by my advice on what springy rod went into what pocket and where the tent pegs should be driven in.

Over the years we have become rather skilled at setting up and breaking down camp and sorting out the division of labours. Broadly, I pack and unpack the car, and my wife makes a temporary home where there was naught but a patch of green.

In the back of our surprisingly capacious Citroën Picasso, I have managed to fit in the new tent, two sleeping bags, an inflatable mattress, a brace of uninflatable pillows, two collapsible tables and a pair of even more collapsible chairs, two cooking stoves with a dozen replacement gas cylinders, a variety of plates, pot and pans and utensils and cooking aides, a washing-up bowl and drying line, a whistling kettle, two lap-top computers, two sets of wellington and hiking boots, two walking staves, the thing that gets obstinate tent pegs out of the ground and a hand axe for foraging or self-defence in more remote areas. Then there is some heavy weather clothing, a couple of hats and caps, a couple of headlamp torches, any number of rolls of lavatory paper, our wash bags and towels and the sports bags containing our supply of clothes.

As usual we have brought at least twice as many books as we could possibly get through in four weeks, and that does not include those on our Kindle e-book readers. As some people still ensure they are wearing clean underwear in case they are run over by a bus, we take too much reading material. Nearly anything is bearable in a foreign country if you have a good book to read.

Also as usual and in spite of the obsessive checking and re-checking the check-list, we (or as my wife says, I) have managed to forget to pack two fairly essential items. One is the pump for our inflatable mattress, and the other my supply of underpants.

My wife can forgive me forgetting the pump, but is convinced that neglecting to pack the dozen pairs of boxer shorts she had laid out on the bed was a deliberate or even subconsciously deliberate omission. She actually believes I have a desire to free myself of all encumbrances beneath my cycling shorts and in the modern parlance, go commando for the entire journey.

She leaves to make enquiries of Serge about the nearest underwear establishment, and I am left with orders to start blowing up the inflatable mattress by mouth.

This attracts some attention and amusement from our neighbours, who all seem to have accommodations complete with king-size or even four-poster beds.

The thing about the French is that they almost never go anywhere on holiday but to another part of their own country. This means their ownership of caravans and increasingly larger and more sophisticated camper vans must be one of the highest in Europe. For sure, those lined up alongside and opposite our little tent look more like spaceships than touring vehicles.

All are parked to catch the sun in the morning and all have their awnings out although it is a cloudy day. It is clear that there is a degree of one-upmanship taking place. One camper has gleaming white spats over the wheels to protect them from the non-existent sun, and the one next to it has a hostess trolley and cocktail bar alongside a dining table which would not look out of place in a proper house. A couple across the path are watching television *al fresco*, while their neighbour ostentatiously works out on an exercise bicycle. A really expensive road bike is fixed to the back of his campervan, and begs the question why he chooses to pedal to nowhere.

As I pause for breath over the still distinctly deflated mattress, a large all-terrain vehicle towing a caravan makes a mess of Serge's artwork and then pulls up alongside the posh campervans. The static cyclist and the couple watching TV pause from their labours to see how adept the driver is at parking. He gets out of his car and confounds them by using a remote control device to steer the caravan into the exact place he wants it.

In response, the man on the immobile bike begins to pedal furiously again, while the man watching TV with his wife regains the upper hand by producing his own remote control and causing the satellite dish on the roof of their camper to rotate. This pleases the operator but earns a sharp word from his wife as she can no longer watch the soap she was enjoying.

Argentan is claimed to be the 6,810th most popular dwelling place in France. That might not sound too promising, but you have to remember that there are coming up for forty thousand communes in France. A commune is an administrative area, and can contain several villages and hamlets. Anyway, I am always suspicious of these 'best place to live in' surveys, as we are never told who the pollsters are and whom they asked. What if they asked the mayor and workers in the local tourist office, or conversely were waiting with their clipboards outside the clubhouse of the local Pessimists Association after a particularly depressing meeting? However Argentan got its ranking, those few members of the population of little more than a thousand we have met seem contented enough, in spite of the impenetrable road system in the centre of town.

Like all French provincial towns, Argentan is ringed with the modern essentials to everyday life. There is the inevitable MacDonald's and other big name fast-food outlets, a giant DIY store, glut of supermarkets and even a drive-through bakery. There is also a giant camping supply store, so the pump problem is quickly resolved.

The underpants issue takes longer.

After going round the same roundabout three times, we find the cleverly concealed entrance to an Intermarché hypermarket, lock up our bikes and head for the underpants section.

Having seen the prices being asked for a pair of designer boxer shorts, I think that the prospect of going commando for the rest of our trip not such a bad one. Normally I buy my underwear at a local boot sale, so am not used to paying a king's ransom for my pants. This is not to say that I opt for second-hand underclothing, but there is a stall where you can pick up packs of factory rejects at less than a pound a pair. This seems eminently reasonable to me for a garment which is hardly ever seen and needs no pockets or zips or other accessories. Here, a single pair of unassuming men's' knickers can cost more than a bottle of very decent Merlot. A packet of designer underpants can come in at more than a bottle of

Champagne.

I wander open-mouthed around the shelves until my wife loses patience and gives me a deadline to find an alternative to the super-expensive varieties. The search goes on until I discover a shelf of bargain basement pants hidden round the corner from the main display as if closer proximity might offend the posh ones. I am delighted to find some packs that are even cheaper than in England at a fiver for six pairs. This is probably because they are made of a flimsy, hopefully stretchable material in a variety of lurid hues. They remind me of the sort of tiny v-shaped swimming trunks popular some years ago which were referred to somewhat coarsely as budgie smugglers.

I grab a couple of packets and suggest my wife takes a look at the ladies' shoe department so she will be distracted and not ask to see my purchase. At the check-out I find my purchases cause a raised eyebrow when I explain that the case of beer is for the warden at the campsite, and the cheese and pants are for me. It is not till I pack the pants in a shopping bag that I realise they are not budgie-smugglers, but the briefest of ladies' knickers.

~

All is at action stations in the town centre as organisers, local police and bar owners make ready for a race passing by this evening. A poster reveals it is not a warm-up for the Tour de France, but a charity event involving local people. It is obviously a big enough occasion to warrant coverage by the local radio station, and a string of loudspeakers surrounding the square are already booming out at peak volume.

Normal French people talk rather quickly; radio presenters talk at around twice the normal velocity. They also like to garner interest and even excitement in what they are saying by raising and dropping the level and tone of their voices a lot. Also the way the loudspeakers are set facing each other around the square, there is a considerable degree of echo and feedback. This means I cannot follow what is happening, but at least all the while the presenters are speaking we will not have to listen to any French pop music.

We find a bar with a terrace fronting on to the square and settle down to watch the fun as a large van draws up and disgorges a dozen men in hi-visibility jackets, trousers and caps. From their armbands we can tell they are stewards. Wearing a uniform can bring about a metamorphosis in the behaviour of men of any nationality, but in France it seems to be more so.

The stewards set to with tape and cones and plastic barriers, and are in full swing when a municipal police car arrives with lights flashing and sirens blaring. The vehicle has to stop short of entering the square as the stewards have blocked off every exit and entrance. An altercation now develops between one of the stewards and one of the policemen, with their colleagues providing back-up arm waving.

From what I can make out, the cause of the row is not the blocking off of all of the routes in and out of town - including presumably the one that the runners will take. What is upsetting both sides is that the stewards are equipped with what look like long-handled table tennis bats with green and red sides. These miniature Stop and Go signs are, the policeman is arguing, to be used by specially trained, accredited and full-time representatives of the commune. Or in other words, he and his colleagues in the *Police Municipale*.

The row hots up as more spectators arrive and move closer to enjoy the altercation. Suddenly, attention is drawn away as the cavalcade that precedes all events of this sort enters the square, bursting through one of the No Entry tapes like the winner of a track event.

The procession is headed by a phalanx of yet more stewards, but these are cycling stewards, keeping to tight formation and all waving aloft the Stop/Go lollipop signs that the argument is about. The policeman sees that he is outgunned, gives a resentful Force Five shrug and retreats to his car.

Behind the cycle outriders is a column of vans, each plastered with posters and advertising placards and logos, and each bearing a loudspeaker. Predictably, each loudspeaker is broadcasting a message from a different sponsor, and added to the echoing announcements from the speakers in the square, cacophony reigns.

The commercial caravan moves on, to be followed by a lone steward. He is walking slowly along the middle of the road, his arms outstretched, He carries a larger and longer handled version of the lollipop signs, and as he flourishes it on each side I am put in mind of an old illustration of Moses parting the Red Sea.

The steward passes through and an expectant murmur runs through the crowd, audible in spite of the radio deejays. Eventually, a lone figure appears in the distance. He is a long and very thin man in tiny shorts and a baggy singlet and a headband. He is even wearing fingerless gloves and jogs with an attitude, so is obviously the local champion and taking the event as well as himself very seriously. Nearing the crowd, he begins running in a very stylised way, which looks copied from the scene in *Chariots of Fire* when the athletes lope along the beach. The trouble is that there is none of the hypnotic music which accompanies the scene in the film, and it is difficult to run in slow motion in real life. After a while, the man gives up and picks up speed and passes through the square. I notice he is getting some compensation by waving to the crowd in slow motion.

A considerable wait, and then the main body of contestants appear. Some are obviously keen amateurs with all the right running gear. Others are clearly joining in for the fun. One man is clad in a holey vest with trousers held up by braces and heavy boots. He has an enormous paunch which moves up and down with every step. As some of the other runners reach out for cups of water to dramatically empty over their heads, the round man slows and comes to a stop outside a bar from where his supporters have been egging him on. As he flops in a chair he is handed a glass of beer and a fag, both of which he goes to work on with relish.

The knot of runners passes through the square, followed by a straggle of competitors, all being herded on by a vintage motor car. It is a Mini-Moke and being driven by a man in a St Bernard dog costume. As it draws level I see that it is in fact a real dog. Then I realise the old British vehicle is a right hand drive and the man at the wheel is obscured by the St Bernard, who is sitting up and enjoying the show.

~

An hour later and the carnival has moved on.

Our appetites sharpened by all the excitement, we have found a Spanish-style restaurant and bar. In the way that all Italian restaurants in France serve only French wine, the menu describes tapas dishes composed entirely of French delicacies. In place of chorizo sausage there are slices of *saucisson*; instead of Manchego cheese from La Mancha there is Camembert from Lower Normandy. Rather than Jamon Serrano, the paper-thin sliced ham is from Bayonne, and in place of tortillas there are *Galettes a la mode Espagnol*.

It has been an interesting if almost bizarre introduction to Argentan, and the evening is made complete when I go to the aid of an elderly English lady who is regarding the menu with some distress.

When I ask if I can help, she gives a delicate shudder and points at a box which explains the customer loyalty scheme. It appears that customers will receive a tampon with every purchase, and ten tampons will earn a gourmand coffee. When I explain that whereas it has only one meaning in English, *tampon* has a variety of meanings in French. In this case it refers to the rubber stamp used to mark the loyalty cards. Hearing this, the lady lets out a small sigh of apparent relief, thanks me for my help and invites us to join her in a glass of wine to celebrate her acquiring a new French word. As she says, at her age she had thought she would have little need of that particular word on either side of the Channel.

You can tell a lot about a campsite from its toilets, and I have seen operating theatres not as deeply cleaned as the one at Argentan.

The tiles on floor and wall glisten like ice crystals. Every surface gleams and the mirrors are so free of the slightest mote or speck that you feel you could climb through them to another, opposing world. Overall, the effect is like those movie scenes where the central character enters a Heaven to be welcomed by a brilliant, gleaming sheen.

And there's more.

One accessory no serious camper travels without is a good supply of toilet paper. Rare is the site with free paper as a standard issue, and you only forget to take a roll with you once.

In Serge's domain, there is not only a full drum of toilet paper in each cubicle, but also a paper towel dispenser which, like the enchanted wine sack, never runs dry.

But even Toilet Heaven must have its drawbacks, and there are two features at this ablutions block which do not find my favour.

One is a stand-and-deliver lavatory, or what the French call a *turque* for reasons it is perhaps best not to go into. It consists of little more than a porcelain tray with a not very big hole in the middle, and a high-level flush cistern with a chain. To help the user position him or herself correctly, the central hole has a raised china footprint on either side. The French seem in general to be poor shots in this regard, and the evidence is often left behind for the next user to discover.

Once upon a time, nearly every bar and public convenience would be equipped with a *turque*; when my wife first encountered one she returned to tell me that someone had stolen the toilet bowl.

The species reached near-extinction with the demise of Edith Piaf, trench coats and trilby hats and delivery vans with corrugated roofs, but has become fashionable again. There are a couple of cubicles with conventional lavatory bowls in this block, but I am drawn to take on the terrible *turque* like a man with vertigo finds it hard to resist standing on the very edge of a cliff or tall building.

Without being indelicate, there are two challenges to take on when using a *turque*. One is that you have to have a near-perfect aim or you will be faced with a sometimes major clearing-up job. The other is to use the flush cistern without getting a soaking. For obvious reasons, the water is delivered to the tray with ferocious velocity, and one has to be nimble to avoid tangential spray of water and other, more noisome substances. This is not easy if you still have your trousers round your ankles. I shall make it my business to take on and defeat the *turque* before we leave Argentan, but for now I must escape the toilet block before I am driven mad by the muzak.

Night and day, 24/7, visitors to the block are subjected to piped music of the worse variety. It comes from a loudspeaker screwed immovably above the entrance door and is, naturally, French in content. Even the French do not like their own music, and radio stations recently staged a revolt against a new ruling by, of all people, the French culture minister. She is trying to impose a restrictive quota on the amount of English-language music aired on all radio stations, and I wish her luck.

My theory with the situation here is that Serge installed the system to ensure campers spend as little time as possible defiling their pristine surroundings.

I also suspect that even he cannot bear exposure to the constant loop of chirpy, infantile warbling, and this morning I caught him wearing earphones and whistling along to an old Beatles hit while swabbing out the showers.

## Suisse Normande

Today we are going to Switzerland, or at least the Normandy version.

*Suisse Normande* straddles the border between Orne and Calvados, and today we will be travelling along the southern half of a circuitous route of around 80 miles.

The term Norman Switzerland came to popularity in the 19th century, and the idea was neither new nor particularly accurate. Apart from the role model there are at least a dozen Little Switzerlands in Europe, and I know of one in Hampshire which consists of no more than a couple of wooded hills.

To be fair, the Norman version is an enchanting place, the landscape in part formed by the eternal meandering of the Orne River. The trail takes a winding route through hills and vales and rocky outcrops, and passes cottages in precarious positions which must be owned by people who also own strong legs, a reliable car or choose to stay in a lot.

## Putanges

We escape from the Argentan no-way system after the third attempt, and take the long straight Roman road due west.

Putanges, or to give it its Sunday-best title, Putanges-Pont-Écrepin, is a pretty little town dating back to the 13th century. The double-barreled name is because, like the region, Putanges is a town of two halves. The original village was sited on the hill overlooking a meander of the Orne, but all that remains of Old Putanges is an ancient manor house, its chapel and cemetery.

The new village grew through iron-working on the banks of the river, and became known when the new 'Swiss Normandy' began to attract tourists. 19th-century Norman writer (and mate of Charles Baudelaire) Gustave Levavasseur was one notable admirer. As he said: 'Everyone knows the admirable little valley where the town of Putanges sits on granite...and the houses seem to be eagles' nests on top of a rock...'

The village of Pont-Écrepin was built on a hill known as La Roche, and has an unusual bell tower in the shape of a candle-snuffer. The subtlety and variety of light on the river and nearby lake has attracted many artists, and there is an annual Painters' Day with events in and around the now joined-up town.

Today is a *jour férié* (bank holiday) so the markets along the route will be well attended. We stop at what looks like a jolly affair and buy some cheese and sausage and bread and try to ignore the glare of the owners of the nearby butchery and baker's shop. Both are brawny men who stand with arms folded resentfully, watching local housewives splash out on items they could get much cheaper in the shops. I don't know why, but street markets always cause normally careful or even frugal Norman women to spend with abandon on a swede which would taste just the same as one bought in the local supermarket. Maybe it is an altruistic gesture to help traditional markets survive and thrive, or maybe they just like to flash the cash in front of their neighbours.

I notice the butcher is talking out of the side of his mouth to his fellow tradesman and pointing with a boning knife at a lady with a large, round loaf in her shopping bag. She is standing at the front of a queue at a van garlanded with pieces of animals, and is in the process of buying what must be an eye-wateringly expensive leg of lamb. It would be interesting to be in the shops when the lady next calls in to see what sort of service she gets, and how fresh is the meat and bread she is offered.

## Lake Rabondages

We move on to a popular tourist attraction and find a suitable picnic spot and viewpoint next to the improbably-named Tahiti restaurant.

Taking advantage of the natural gorge and basin, the huge artificial lake was created in 1959 and holds six billion cubic litres and covers 95 hectares. In this landlocked department it is a popular haunt for water sports enthusiasts, and ringed by some impressive houses which must be valued almost as highly as a flat above a chip shop in Clapham.

After fantasising about what it would be like to own a home with its own landing jetty, we continue our journey, then mistakenly turn off the route and find ourselves transported to the film set of the latest re-make of *The Three/Four Musketeers*.

A turreted manor house of grim granite appears to be floating on a sea of mist rising from a small lake. There is a causeway to the island on which the *manoir* sits, and nearby is a chapel and cemetery. At any minute we expect a horse-drawn carriage to appear and rattle across the bridge, perhaps escorted or even pursued by a sword-wielding rider wearing a big hat with an even bigger feather in it.

The grandness of the building comes from the tradition in feudal France that the family château would go to the eldest son, while the younger brother would have to put up with the farm. To soften the blow, the farm would be beefed up with witch's hat towers and all sorts of twiddly bits and called a *manoir*. This is where we get the word 'manor' for any sumptuous English country house.

Anywhere in the Home Counties, this wonderful old building would be owned by a Russian oligarch or overpaid soccer star and have its own underground gym, cinema and nightclub. Here it stands sadly but defiantly alone, its windows and magnificently arched entranceway boarded over with cheap deal planking.

Making a note of the exact satnav reference for when we scoop the Euro-Millions pot, we look once more at the abandoned house, sigh, and return to Little Switzerland.

## La Roche d'Oëtre

On through the gorges of St-Aubert and past the 'hidden' village of Saint-Philbert-sur-Orne. This is a thinly-populated part of a thinly populated area, with just the odd dwelling-place or agricultural building clinging to the steep hillsides. At a high point with stunning views across the valley, we spot a little cottage in a sea of grass and meadow flowers. It looks as if it could easily fit into an alpine setting, with a milkmaid or even an outstretched-armed Julie Andrews about to appear from round the corner of the old wooden barn. The three goats watching us from the garden certainly look at home.

Now we enter a land of crags, with giant vertical faces of granite lining our route, and all at once before us lay The Rock.

La Roche d'Oëtre is part of what is said to be the oldest hill in France, though I do not see how they can know that. Our leaflet also informs us that La Roche is one of the most prestigious belvederes in the country. Having looked it up before we started our journey, I know that the word means the same in French and English, and describes 'an open-sided roof terrace, gazebo, turret, tower, pavilion or cupola designed and located so as to look out at a beautiful view'. I have to agree that, prestigious or not, there is a stunning view from this particular belvedere.

The Roche d'Oëtre is a sort of Mecca or at least a magnet for climbers, and the car park is busy with mostly young, fit-looking people putting on or taking off climbing gear. I know that the whole area of the Suisse Normande is often awash with walkers and even cyclists who would presumably find the mountain stages of the Tour de France a doddle.

We fleetingly consider having a go at some impromptu climbing, then think better of it and head for the terraced bar and brasserie which clearly offers customers a very prestigious belvedere.

~

Sitting on the departmental border, Pont d'Ouilly marks the point where the Suisse Normande trail is claimed by Calvados. We will stay faithful to the Orne version, so head off westwards through the valley of the Noireau river past lines of granite escarpments and meandering streams feed pleasingly photogenic water mills.

Suddenly, a huge rust-coloured shape swoops down and across the windscreen. It is the wrong colour for an eagle and far too far north but is certainly a sizeable bird of prey. The magnificent creature pulls out of its dive and levels off at no more than a couple of feet from the ground. It flies with steady and slow flaps in front of the car, its wingtips almost as far apart as our wing mirrors.

I have heard several explanations from French countrymen for this bemusing behaviour. One is that the larger raptors swoop on cars in isolated places to see if they are worth attacking. Another is that they have learned that the engine noise will disturb and send up smaller birds and rabbits from the hedgerows and provide a meal on the wing. A tipsy farmer I met in a bar even claimed that the bigger birds of prey had very small brains and thought that cars of a suitable colour were possible mates. As our Picasso is a virulent shade of turquoise I think the only bird looking for love which might take a fancy to us would be a peacock.

~

We cruise up hill and down into vale and past sparkling streams and flower-strewn meadows and giant corridors of rugged escarpments. If it is possible to become sated with such a rich feast of landscaping variety we must be nearing that point.

We pass by Athis-de-l'Orne, distinguished by being the largest commune in its canton and having two other rivers as well as the one in its name. This is perhaps the reason that its coat of arms features three ducks waddling across a chevroned shield.

Then we turn eastwards on the home run, and I fall into a common trap the authorities like to leave for visitors. The route will be marked more than liberally, then the directional signs will disappear at a point where a change of direction is needed. I take my pick at a junction presenting no less than five choices and we end up in the middle of the middle of nowhere.

Reversing back up a dead-end track and smiling apologetically at an outraged gaggle of geese, I find a metalled road and we arrive in what appears to be an abandoned village. Or at least one where time has stood still for a couple of hundred years.

It is not unusual to see no sign of life in a Norman village, especially at lunchtime. But this place lacks all indicators of habitation. There is no bar or post office or convenience store, and no road signs or markings. No children play in the street, there are no parked cars, and most of the houses look as if they have not been updated since they were built. Then my wife observes that there is no sign of an electricity supply. This is most unusual, as the French like to be artistically creative with water pipes and power cables and give them a high profile.

This village reminds me of a tourist attraction where all signs of modernity have been hidden and tourists can tramp around the cobbled streets and see how things never were. These are not uncommon in France, but where are the visitors or places for their cars and coaches to park? If it is a tourist attraction it is a very unsuccessful one.

As we reach the end of the narrow road, the door on the last house in the terrace opens and a very old man appears on the doorstep. He stands and watches us pass by but makes no response to my wife's smile and wave. I see in the mirror that he watches us for a moment, then turns and shuffles back into the house.

Discussing the mystery as we drive away, my wife says the old man may have been expecting a visitor. I agree but think there may be several other explanations. Either passers-by are so rare that he came out just to watch us go by, or he is the only remaining occupant and was feeling lonely. Also, I venture, he appeared to be dressed in clothing from another century. As my wife says, perhaps what I took for tights were merely long johns as the old chap had not bothered to put his trousers on.

I am not so sure, and prefer to think we have somehow travelled through a time warp and seen a village as it really was a hundred or more years ago. Or perhaps not.

## Flers

We are still discussing the mystery of the abandoned village when we reach the outskirts of the pleasant town of Flers, where the route is blocked. Cars have been carefully parked to create a bottleneck, loudspeakers burp and whine and bunting is being draped over trees and lampposts. From the banners, it looks like a bicycle race, rally or even some sort of strike about the rights of pedallers is being set up. The French are very casual about blocking off main roads for fairs, carnivals and markets, and my theory is that this is because of all the practice they get with strikes, protests and demonstrations.

Cycle racing is of course very big in France and some of the related events resemble the gatherings of Star Trek fanatics. This one looks as if it includes a competition for the cycling jersey of the most revolting hue and worn by the most unsuitable person. Milling around on the road ahead are dozens of men wearing day-glow cycling tops, and hundreds more are browsing at stalls selling bicycle parts, clothing, literature and general accessories. There is a marked absence of women, and some of the men look as if they have not been astride a bike for many years. Rather like beer-bellied soccer fans choosing to wear their team's soccer shirt to a match, cycle racing fans often sport tops with their heroes names emblazoned on the back. Everywhere, Lycra strains across ample paunches and some jerseys are so stretched and distorted that the lettering is unreadable.

In contrast to the well-fed fans, the actual cyclists look like they have not had a square meal for years; there seems not an ounce of fat on their whippet-like bodies, and their skin-tight costumes emphasise the lack of spare flesh.

About forty of the contestants sit astride bicycles which are probably worth more than our car, and all are concentrating on looking mean and magnificent. All wear plastic helmets which appear to have been melted and stretched out to an often ridiculously elongated point as the back. All wear slanting dark glasses, and fingerless gloves, and all are scowling for the benefit of the fans taking their photos.

I am all in favour of these sort of events, but I can see that we are going to be held up for a considerable time if we do not take action.

Consequently, I slip on the high-visibility waistcoat that the law requires every car to carry, grab the gingham check tablecloth we used for the picnic on Lake Rabodanges and open the sun roof.

Then I clamber on to the seat, standing with my hands on the front of the roof like a would-be tank commander. My wife puts on the hazard warning lights and sounds the horn, and I begin to wave the table cloth and shout meaningless but urgent-sounding appeals.

As our car is of a French make and I am making such a fuss, nobody appears to notice our British licence plate or that the steering wheel is on the wrong side. Used to this sort of official brouhaha, the crowd parts to let us through. I give a nod of encouragement at the competitors, then drape the tablecloth around my shoulders and pose like the statue of Napoleon pointing across the Channel to the enemy. In moments we are through and back on track for dinner in Argentan.

~

We have spent some reflective time at the tourist office, looking at the grainy, enlarged black-and-white photographs of the town after it was almost totally destroyed by Allied bombing. In one, an old lady in black stands amongst the rubble, looking towards the camera as if trying to find someone to tell her how and why this could happen.

Free French fighters were amongst the wave after wave of Allied planes which reduced the centre of the ancient town to rubble and killed hundreds of civilians along with the enemy.

One story of hope amongst the carnage and cruelty told us by our guide is of the young German soldier dispatched by an

SS officer to find and kill all the local clergy. The soldier found the curé of Argentan, but rather than shoot him, he laid down his rifle, knelt and asked for benediction. The story concludes with the young soldier deserting and setting out to return home, and it would be nice to think he made it and lived a long and useful life.

# Teurgoule

If Normans are proud of *Tripes de Caen*, they are almost insanely possessive of the rice pudding.

*Tergoule*, *teurgoule* or *tourgoule* allegedly originates (they say) from Lower Normandy, where it was a popular dish at fetes and other social occasions. It is not recorded if rice pudding with a burned skin on top was a favourite of William the Conqueror or travelled over with the Normans in 1066, but the recipe is identical to what was regularly served up in millions of English households in my childhood.

The name is supposed to come from Old Norman for 'twist mouth' which was said to happen to anyone tasting it because of the spiciness of the dish, though unless the recipe has changed, I find that very unlikely.

For sure there is an association formed specifically to pay reverence to the dish, and it has a name almost as long as the amount of time they like to keep their rice puddings in the oven. *The Confrérie des gastronomes de Teurgoule et de Fallue de Normandie* meet regularly to praise the ambrosiacal pudding, parade in their cloaked costumes, and hold a yearly teurgoule-making competition.

## Ingredients

2 teaspoons vanilla sugar
175g caster sugar
175g short grain (pudding) rice
2 litres *raw milk or full fat fresh milk
1 pinch ground cinnamon

## Method

Pre-heat the oven to $150^0$C Gas mk II.
In a large baking dish, mix together the sugar, vanilla sugar, rice, milk and cinnamon.

Put in the oven and stir after twenty minutes so the sugar will not gather at the bottom of the dish.
Continue baking for 4-5 hours until a nice brown skin has formed on the top.

*'Raw' milk is just what it sounds like, and what we all used to drink almost straight from the cow. In short, it has not been pasteurised or homogenised or otherwise interfered with. Some extol its virtue, others say it can be dangerous. The choice is yours.

# Bocage Ornais

Officially, the Orne is divided into three districts, forty townships and five hundred and five municipalities. In everyday use, most Ornaise prefer to use the seven older and more romantic-sounding divisions.

Yesterday we were in the Suisse Normande, and today we will be following the Pear Route around the Bocage Ornaise. This area occupies the south-west of the department, and as well as pride in its fruit, the brochures claim this to be Sir Lancelot du Lac country.

The gallant knight and king cuckolder's funeral *stele* is to be found at the town of St Fraimbault-de-Lassay. In practice and as with Little Switzerland, there are at least a dozen places in Normandy and Brittany claiming to be the birth, death or burial places of Lancelot and other Knights of the Round Table.

Also and if you want to be strictly accurate about the location of the alleged deathplace of Lancelot, St Fraimbault-de-Lassay is over the border in Mayenne. But, as with the *Suisse Normande,* I see no problem with two departments claiming the same attraction.

*Common in Brittany where they have a penchant for standing stones, a stele is any slab in stone or wood erected as a monument or to mark some event or even territory. They have long been used as funerary objects, and you could technically say that the traditional British gravestone is a stele.*

~

Duped by the road maze at Argentan into touring the outskirts, I note that the roundabout artists have been hard at work.

Local authorities like you to know that they are not soulless bureaucrats and that they can appreciate and demonstrate their *avant-garde* and arty heritage. They do this in the most conspicuous if unlikely places, and roundabouts make the perfect open-air galleries. When I first saw a collection of rusting metal pieces apparently dumped in a heap on a big roundabout on the outskirts of a major town, I thought that it was a cheeky example of fly-tipping. Then someone told me it was art, and that the installation reflected the chaos of the creative mind.

There is inevitably a degree of one-upmanship about what and how much you can get on to your roundabouts and how striking the installation will look. This overkill also serves the purpose of distracting drivers from where they want to go.

Some of these monumental works of street art reflect local history or industry, so you might see an artistically posed fishing boat or giant carrot just when you least expect it. I once saw a rusting, window and wheel-less car on a roundabout outside a major motor-manufacturing plant. It was there for months before anyone realised that it was actually an abandoned vehicle which had mounted the roundabout and burst into flames while the drunken driver was trying to escape from a pursuing police car.

## Ferté Macé

Funny name, funny town.

Ferté Macé is dominated by the twin towers of its church, which makes it seem you have momentary double vision. It is also distinguished by having a racetrack disguised as a traffic-calming measure.

There are no pavements, and a chicane is created by strategically-placed planters and litter bins. This is obviously meant to slow traffic down, but in fact encourages motorists to emulate their favourite F1 drivers and get from one end to the other against the clock.

The town is also noteworthy for one of the inmates of a military detention centre there in World War One. American poet E.E. Cummings was also an eminent painter and essayist, and, like Ernest Hemmingway, elected to drive an ambulance in foreign parts during the war. He and a Yankee friend were heard expressing anti-war sentiments in a local bar, so were arrested and detained on a charge of espionage.

Another curiosity is that there are large welcome signs in French and German, but none that I can see in English.

Perhaps it is just an omission.

I have often asked Norman bar owners and restaurateurs if they do value Teutonic visitors over British. Some of the more candid ones said they do, but it is because the Germans are always over-polite and leave much bigger tips than the English.

## Le Forêt d'Andaines

Whether or not the legends of fairies and hermits and supernatural creatures said to be residing there are true, the Forest of Andaines is, to say the least, atmospheric. It covers more than a hundred thousand hectares, and the deeper one penetrates, the more other-worldly it becomes. We left the main road miles back and have arrived at one of the smallest and strangest of chapels.

Dedicated to Ste Genevieve, it seems more Celtic than Catholic, and no bigger than a roadside shrine. The exterior is covered with carved fertility symbols and hobgoblin-type leering faces, and it stands in a completely bizarre setting. Leading down the slope and deeper into the forest are a series of armchairs and sofas carved from the same solid granite as the chapel. They are interspersed with carvings and three-dimensional representations of fantastic creatures and overtly phallic symbols which are definitely more Pagan than Christian.

Beyond these curiosities is a stone lectern, which stands before a low, stone table and looks like a sacrificial slab for use by Druids with very short legs. A sign above the slab says it is the *Lit de la Gione*. I can find no reference to Gione in even ancient French, and the nearest translation is 'hero' in the Eastern European language of Aromanian.

I think I hear a low snuffling grunt in the undergrowth by the Bed of Gione and suggest we get on our way. With a distinct feeling of being watched, we leave the clearing and the clearly enchanted forest and head for Normandy's only proper spa town.

# Bagnoles-de-l'Orne

If ever there was a place where you could imagine Hercule Poirot mincing down the steps of a very grand hotel in his white suit, high collar and panama, it is here.

There are many hotels with spa facilities in the region, but Bagnoles-de-l'Orne is famed for its hydrotherapic baths.

The habit of taking the local waters internally or externally is said to go back to Medieval times, and there is, as usual, a legend to explain how it all began. Believing his beloved old horse Rapide was at the end of his days, the local liege lord Hugues de Tessé abandoned him in the Forest of Andaines, which I have to say is not an uncommon practice in rural France when a pet or uneatable working animal is on its last legs.

Imagine the surprise of the seigneur when Rapide appeared on his doorstep as hale and hearty as he had been a decade before. Without a trace of resentment, the horse led its master to the waters of Bagnoles, where the lord took a drink and also became reinvigorated. From then on, the punters flocked to the spa to regain their youth and vitality. To further understand the popularity of regaining lost vigour, you have to remember that this was centuries before Viagra was invented.

Another legend has it that an aged monk was so rejuvenated by taking the waters that he performed an amazing leap across the highest rock in town. That rock is still known as *Le Saut de Capucin*, or The Monk's Leap.

Nowadays, the spa is centred round a lake formed by the river Vée before it travels through a deep gorge in the Forest of Andaines.

The French are Europe's champion medicine-takers by a long chalk, and are not unknown for a tendency towards hypochondria. This ensured the growth and continuing popularity of Bagnoles, and it certainly looks and feels like a recuperation centre for the wealthy. The town is packed with shops selling cures for every sort of ailment and indisposition, and the pricey hotels provide comfort and succour for those who enjoy bad health. As Las Vegas caters for those who want to gamble, Bagnoles-de-l'Orne caters for those who want to spend their money on their physical wellbeing...or flaunting their lack of it.

There is an air of affluence everywhere, and even the dogs parade with their noses in the air. In the immaculately manicured grounds around the lake, old men dodder and ladies of a certain age recline wanly on benches beside the lake to read or just concentrate on looking fragile.

For those who wish to be a little more active, there is an opulently domed casino and regular tours of sites with connections to the Arthurian legends. There are also some corking *art deco* buildings to inspect. I could enjoy a couple of weeks of R&R here, but only if I had notched up a best-seller to pay for it.

As we decide against lunching at a local restaurant where the daily specials are beyond our budget, a lady in a flowing white dress and a huge hat steps out into the road, preceded by her immaculately coiffed standard poodle. In most French towns I know, there would have been an eruption of honking and imprecations, but here the traffic stopped respectfully to let her cross. I don't know who she is or if she was a national or local celebrity, but we got the feeling Bagnoles appreciates and quite likes posh people with lots of money and the most haughty of airs.

## Ceaucé

More tales of the paranormal.

It is said that the little town of Ceaucé was the last sorcerer hotspot in France. Some say it still is, but it seems a pretty innocuous and un-spellbinding place.

We have been this way before and last time visited a bar set in the 1930s. This is not a trendy retro design feature, but the period when the furnishings and fitments were new.

These sorts of establishments are common in rural France and usually presided over by a patron who grew up on the premises. For that reason the bar feels more like a home which allows visitors, and we like this.

The man behind this bar is in his seventh decade and has many tales to tell of how the town was in the old days, though it does not appear to have changed much. Denys has no children, so plans to sell up and buy a flat with all mod cons in the town centre. Unfortunately, a British customer told him what the business and building would be worth in London, so he has set his sights far too high. He is bitterly disappointed with the more realistic valuation given him by the local estate agent, so has insisted on setting his own price. I fear he will be standing behind the bar for a while, unless there is a dramatic change to French property prices.

With a population of little more than a thousand, Ceaucé is typical of many hundreds of small French towns. It merits no more than a single line in any of the references I can find, and is best known for the distance it is from more celebrated towns. It can't be nice to know that your home town is regarded as a marker on the road to somewhere else. Ceaucé is, the guide books and sites tell us, only 55 kilometres from the birthplace of William the Conqueror, 45 kilometres from the great castle at Fougeres, and just up the road from the ancient hilltop town of Domfront.

~

On route to one of the most touristy places in Orne, we pass through a hamlet composed almost entirely of ancient *colombage* cottages and barns. For those unfamiliar with the term, 'colombage' is the building style we like to call half-timbering...or mock-Tudor when it is a modern reincarnation of a very ancient type of building. Basically, it is a framework of roughly dressed timber which has the gaps filled in with a mix of mud and straw upon which your cattle and pigs had peed (it helped with the waterproofing).

Nowadays, people go weak at the knees just from looking at this early style of building, which might be genetic memory or nostalgia for a time that never was. Whatever the reason, I cannot see people flocking to pose for photographs in front of a block of mid-20th-century mansion flats in a couple of hundred years. I don't suppose it was all that much fun living in a wood and mud hovel in those times, but have to agree that, of all the ways you can build a house, this one wins the prize for making people go 'oooooh.'

Across the Channel, these sorts of villages and buildings would be lived in by retired colonels and city whizz-kids and there would be all sorts of ferociously strict preservation orders governing the maintenance requirements and banning any sort of changes, or as the owners might say, improvements.

Here, gable ends which have fallen down over the centuries have been replaced by crudely cemented-together breeze blocks, and rusty sheets of corrugated iron have taken the place of thatch. It doesn't look very pretty, but lends the hamlet an air of reality and sense of continuity when you know that the same sort of people - and sometimes even the same families - are living in the homes as built them.

~

So far we have seen more advertisements for pear products than the fruit itself.

Crudely home-made and slick professional roadside notices invite us to drop in and buy bottles of pear wine, pear cider and even pear brandy. Although this is the Pear Route and we are in Orne, one can also pick up farm-made Calvados apple brandy and *pommeau*, which is the result of mixing apple juice with apple brandy.

Then suddenly we are in serious pear-growing territory. On either side of the road, row after arrow-straight row of small fruit trees disappear into the distance. Pears were known to prehistoric hunter-gatherers in the form of wild fruit which was to become known as *poirasse*. The first references to processing the fruit occur as far back as the 4th century. There is a renowned centre of production at our final destination, and it specialises in perry, or 'Norman Champagne'. It is also known as 'Champagne for the poor'.

# Domfront

Like Normandy, Domfront is a place of two halves.

At ground level it is a modern-day, bustling town, much like any other with its chromium-and-plate-glass-fronted rows of shops and bars and offices.

Looking down on all the hoot and toot with silent contempt is the old town, haunted still by the souls of ancient rulers and their servants in the Church who kept the common folk and their betters in order.

Set high on a lone hill and looking out across a great plain in all directions, Domfront was a rallying point for the dispossessed and youngest son of William the Conqueror. He was to become Henry I, ruler of all the Anglo-Norman dominions.

Nowadays, the population level is a little less than 4000, which must be no more than a fraction of the tourists who wend their way up the winding road to the old town every year.

We park outside the imposing town hall and note that there are more British licence plates surrounding us than any other variety, including French. In front of the *mairie* is a row of gleaming white posts on which fly French, Norman, EEC and German flags. I do not want to get a thing about another notable omission, so assume the Union Jack is away being cleaned or repaired.

We buy croissants at a picture-postcard bakery (which in fact sells picture postcards of itself) and sit on the battlements and look out across the countryside, imagining what it must have been like to be a sentinel on duty here on a cold and blustery night.

Before checking out the ruined castle, we walk through the cobbled streets past ancient dwellings which seem to be holding each other up. It does not jar that some of the oldest and grandest homes now have busy restaurants and bars and shops on their ground floors. For me it makes the town live to see a couple eating *moules* at a bench table in a cobbled street in the shadow of a giant Dalek.

The previous incarnation of the Church of St Julian was built in 1744, but, considered insufficient for its position and needs, was torn down and replaced by a weirdly-designed ferro-concrete monster in 1926. Art Deco it ain't, and nobody amongst the hundreds of tourists are bothering to take photos. Inside it is equally garish and evokes thoughts of a Greek Orthodox place of worship rather than any sort of Norman church I have seen.

~

I do not know if the people of Argentan are more abstemious or anti-social than elsewhere in France, but pubs in the town centre are very thin on the ground.

Research during our initial visit shows that Argentan has little more than a handful of betting shops, tabacs and straightforward bars to serve a sizeable population. This is unusual even in provincial France. Even more noticeable is how many of the bars close as early as 8pm, and this in summertime. It is one of the few places where I could go on a pub crawl and remain resolutely sober.

Thankfully the sort-of Spanish bar is open, so we have a traditional Iberian meal of *chevre chaud* (warm goat's cheese salad) followed by an entrecote steak which has been merely shown the pan and now lies submerged beneath a small lake of very flavorsome Camembert sauce. As a concession to vegetables, there is as usual a mountain of chips. The only other diners are a party of youngsters, who are showing their willingness to integrate with the rest of the EEC by having the special Franco-Spanish tapas board with ice-cold mugs of local cider.

# Lost & Forgotten Bread

When we were considering puddings at the Spanish bar, I thought I heard the waiter say he had lost our bread. He was actually recommending what has become a very upmarket pudding with humble roots.

*Pain perdu* was originally a simple way of using up stale bread, which the French get a lot of because it is unpreserved and so has a very short eat-by window. When in France, we Brits tend to buy huge loaves and get stuck with the granite they become by afternoon. French families will visit the *boulangerie* up to three times a day, buying smaller items like a *baguette* or even a really skinny *ficelle* (literally *'string')* but even the most astute buyers have left-overs. A traditional Gallic way of making stale bread more than palatable is known by us as French Toast. This is made by dipping slices of bread into beaten egg and frying them. Nowadays in France, *Pain Perdu* can be a bit more complex and either sweet or savoury or both at the same time. The simple dish has been elevated to a very haughty *haute cuisine* level in some expensive French restaurants. Here's a good example:

## Ingredients

Quarter of a teaspoon of fresh lime zest
3 tablespoons of sugar
A tablespoon of lime juice
A pint of strawberries, hulled and chopped in half
2 large eggs
2 teaspoons of vanilla extract
4 thick slices of stale-ish *brioche or French-style bread
2 ounces of blanched and chopped almonds
2 tablespoons of unsalted butter
A pinch of salt
Some whipped cream

## Method

Rub the zest into a tablespoon of the sugar, stir in the lime juice and strawberries.

In a shallow dish, whisk together the eggs, remaining sugar, vanilla and salt. Now whisk in the milk, add the slices of bread/brioche, turn to coat both sides and then leave to soak for ten minutes.

Place the almonds in another bowl and melt the butter in a suitable frying pan.

Dip one side of each slice into the almonds and add to the pan, nut-side down.

Cook until the almonds are golden brown, then flip the slices and cook the other side until brown.

Finally, put the slices on plates, cover with strawberries and add lashings of cream.

*Brioche is a firm French favourite and is a very light and rich bread with a texture and taste we would liken to a bun. It has a high egg and butter content and is technically known as a vienneoiserie. In this category would be included croissants and the delightful pain aux raisins.*

# Pays d'Auge

Early morning and another traumatic encounter with the Turkish toilet. I am assisted from the cubicle with trousers round ankles by a sympathetic man who is also our new neighbour.

Another usually positive aspect of camping is that you quickly get to know those with whom you share intimate moments. Tent walls are thin and there are no secrets between people sharing an ablutions block, eating in the open and washing their dirty underwear in public.

Our neighbour arrived on site after dark in spite of Serge's curfew, and we invited him and his wife to join us for a nightcap. Julian told us he is well over eighty and regretfully coming to the end of his caravanning days. He and his wife have spent all their lives on the island of Jersey, which is why they like to get away and enjoy the freedom of the open road. He bought the French-made caravan nearly half a century ago, and it must be worth more as a vintage model than it was brand new.

Julian was a teenager during WWII, and I asked him how life was in the only part of Britain to be occupied. He said that at first the islanders had to put up with swaggering, arrogant officers and loutish troops, and it was humiliating to have to make way for the invaders. Things got better when Hitler made his disastrous move on Russia, and the sometimes brutish troops were replaced by old men and boys, some of who were barely older than himself. They had been conscripted, so had no more enthusiasm for their being there than their unwilling hosts.

Our neighbour has some fascinating tales to tell about the Channel Islands. Another bonus to camping in close proximity to strangers is that you quickly get to know people you would otherwise never have met. Many have absorbing tales to tell. As my wife says, this is my excuse for visiting so many bars and striking up conversations with people I do not know and will never meet again.

~

Today we will be visiting the east of the department, following a circuit through an area known for its apples, old stone buildings, water mills and France's favourite cheese.

The Pays D'Auge straddles the departments of Orne and Calvados, and is notable for its lack of *bocage*. We have not passed a hedge for miles, and on either side of the road lay great swathes of cereal, the miniature forests of wheat swaying in unison in the breeze.

Rape seed is another intensively produced crop here, and I think it would not be a good place to live for a hay fever sufferer.

We drive on across the treeless landscape, telephone and electricity posts lining our route and on them birds of prey waiting patiently for the chance of a take-away meal.

As we near the border with Calvados, the colombage and thatched roof count rises rapidly. Fresh flowers are knotted into the ridge of some of the thatches, which is an old Norman tradition. It is said the practice dates back to Pagan times and was an offering to the gods of nature to ensure there would always be food and drink in the home.

Soon, the oceans of cereal give way to orchards, and the *bocage* reappears. The lines of apple trees are ripe with fruit and when autumn comes they will be gathered in to start the ancient process of creating cider and apple brandy. Most of the fruit will be sold to local *cidreries* and distilleries, but some will be kept for home-brew use.

Even the smallest cottages have their own mini-orchards, and often a sheep or solitary milk cow grazing beneath the branches. I wonder if the inhabitants have got used to the sight of a cow looking through their living room window, or still appreciate what they have. Many of the cottages have smart new cars parked in the yard and TV aerials or satellite dishes on the roofs, but it is good to know that some aspects of rural living have remained unchanged.

## Crouttes

If there is a middle of nowhere, it cannot be far from Crouttes.

We have not seen a car or human being for twenty minutes since leaving the main road to take a look at the Priory of St Michel. As tradition dictates, the official brown sign recommending an historic site entices the driver from the road, then it is anyone's guess how far or in which direction the place is.

Finally, we see an impressive building which fits the bill, but is mostly hidden behind a high wall. The huge gates are locked and barred, but there is a large notice offering a B&B service rather than Matins. This means the priory is now in private hands, or the holy order there is making a few bob on the side from the tourist trade.

Like the priory, Crouttes appears closed for the day. There is no sign of life about the outlying homes or the handful of immaculately-maintained colombage cottages in the centre of the village. Somehow, nearly 300 people have found a reason to be elsewhere, or choose to remain indoors at the time of our visit.

The only human form is on constant guard duty at the war memorial. Here stands a life-sized statue of a soldier from the Great War. He is painted in garish hues of pink and blue and red, which somehow makes what it represents more poignant. We stand and look at the handful of names engraved on the stone slab, which show how even the remotest and smallest dwelling places in France made their own sacrifice.

## Vimoutiers

A shade over three thousand people call Vimoutiers home, which makes it a busy town in this neck of the woods. Like so many places in this region, it has an eventful and at times violent past. In 1040, the Duke of Normandy died here of poisoning. During the Battle of Normandy, the town was destroyed by Allied bombardment, resulting in the death of 220 local people. A witness to the onslaught was a German Tiger tank, now standing on the outskirts as a permanent reminder of what took place here on the 14th of June 1944.

Most French towns have a statue or two of local dignitaries on show outside the civic offices. Vimoutiers has a life-size statue of a cow. Her name is Ratisfaite and she was created by a renowned sculptor as a tribute to a classic Normandy dairy breed. Across the way from Ratisfaite is a statue of the woman who came up with one of the nation's greatest cheese.

Marie Fontaine was born at Crouttes in 1761. She married Jacques Haral in 1785, and so began one of the great cheese dynasties. We shall now visit the village that gave its name to that most iconic of French cheeses, admired and eaten in more than 150 countries around the world.

## Camembert

Although we have been travelling around France for decades, this is the first time we have been to Camembert, and it is fascinating to see a village sign with the same name as a famous cheese.

Though Marie Haral made it famous, the credit for Camembert cheese goes to an irascible priest who was fleeing from the mobs of Paris in the days of The Terror. The story goes that he gave Marie some advice on how to best mature cheese, and her experiments in the village resulted in the unique taste and texture which sets it apart from the other 300-odd French soft cheeses.

The big breakthrough came with the arrival of a train link to Paris in 1850, meaning the capital's *beau monde* could buy the newly fashionable cheese six hours after it left the village. The seal of approval came when Napoleon III stopped off at Camembert on his way to a day's racing at the nearby course of Haras du Pin. Louis-Napoléon Bonaparte was so taken with a sample that he ordered Camembert to be served every day at the Tuileries Palace.

The next stage in the making of a legend was the development of the distinctive circular wooden boxes which could keep the cheese fresh for much longer. Then it was discovered that spraying the cheese with an early form of penicillin would create a thick, protective crust. A final act of near-genius in marketing terms was to donate a million cheeses to cheer up the gallant soldiers in the trenches in 1915.

Nowadays, Camembert is said to be the jewel in Normandy's crown and the region is very proud of its world-wide fame. One of the most memorable if bemusing advertising slogans in the museum went so far as to claim that a day without Camembert was like a beautiful woman with only one eye.

After a most generous sampling session in the Camembert museum, we drive away replete, and content with the knowledge that we have been consuming a health food. According to the manufacturers, eating a raw milk product with a 46 percent fat content bestows all sorts of medical benefits and who are we to argue with the experts?

*Technical note: Though nobody outside the top echelons of the company is privy to the exact recipe, it is known that two litres of milk go into making every small round of Camembert.*

*The curdling process is aided by the addition of an enzyme from the stomach of a calf, then the embryo cheese is shaped and bathed in salt water. It is eventually sprayed with penicillin to create the fungus which becomes the crust. The distinctive ridges on the crust come from the wire racks on which the cheese matures (or, as the makers say, 'blooms') for two weeks. The maturing process is still continuing when it leaves the factory, and with the aid of the breathable box the contents should reach prime condition in around two weeks.*

*As we learned during the tour of the museum, it is still argued that eating Camembert is a healthy pastime, and up to the 1950s a regular dose was still being prescribed for people with stomach disorders.*

# Camembert Croquettes

Not only does Camembert taste so good straight from the box, it is also surprisingly versatile in adding flavour to a whole raft of dishes and recipes. As a sauce with or without peppercorns it gives a real zing to the blandest of meats, and is even served as a sweet when baked and drizzled with honey.

One of our favourite and simplest ways of enjoying Camembert as a cooked dish is putting it in the oven and warming it up to near-melting point. It is wonderful in this form as a spread on crusty bread or biscuit.

If you want to take a little more trouble, this is a traditional and corking way to eat the great Norman cheese:

## Ingredients

I round of Camembert (not too ripe)
2 eggs
Some crème fraîche
A finely chopped onion
A quarter of a litre of dry cider
Some flour
Some butter
Some breadcrumbs
Some Cayenne pepper
Some nutmeg
Some seasoning
Some lemon juice

## Method

### For the Sauce Normande:

Fry the chopped onion in butter until golden.
Add 30g flour and the same again of butter.

Work with a wooden spatula, and when the roux is cooked after one minute, add the dry cider and beat the mixture thoroughly until thickened.

Add salt and cayenne pepper and a pinch of nutmeg.

Away from the heat, incorporate a quarter of a litre of the crème fraîche and a dash of lemon juice.

For the croquettes:

In a bowl, crush the Camembert with a fork.

Mix in three tablespoons of the Sauce Normande to soften, then mix in some more crème fraîche.

Beat the eggs in another bowl.

Now shape the croquettes, dip them in the beaten egg and roll in the flour and then the breadcrumbs.

Fry in hot oil until they are a golden brown.

Drain on kitchen paper and serve with a *Normandy-style salad.

*In Normandy, a salad is often no more than some crispy lettuce leaves liberally coated with good olive oil. If you want to be a little more creative, you can jazz it up with apple rings, walnut pieces, some cider vinegar, lemon juice, nutmeg and the almost inevitable crème fraîche.*

## Pays d'Ouche

Today we are on an extended tour through three adjoining areas of the Orne.

We began in the Pays d'Ouche, which sounds like a Scotsman in pain if you say it properly in the local dialect.

Ouche occupies a small area in the top right-hand corner of the department. Apart from its unusual name, it is renowned for its lakes, castles, abbeys and other assorted religious institutions. We have also found it a very hospitable area.

Passing through the pretty village of Villers-en-Ouche, we saw a sign advertising a XVIIth-century *château* open to the public. Arriving at a set of very grand gates, we were disappointed to find a notice announcing that the premises were temporarily closed.

The gates being unlocked, I parked the car and persuaded my wife that we should sneak in and at least take an outside look. We walked down the seemingly endless tree-lined drive trying to look as if we were on familiar territory. When poking around somewhere where I should not be, I have found it best to try and look as if I have every right to be there.

You only have to watch *The Great Escape* and other prisoners-of-war-on-the-run movies to know that an air of confidence is key to carrying off any deception. In some cases and if feeling particularly bolshie, I try and look as if I am part of or even own the establishment. It is a tactic which deeply embarrasses my wife, but it has got us out of some sticky moments.

In this case, any attempt to look as if I was on official business would have been undermined by my long shorts and Superman tee-shirt, so I opted for posing as a gardener.

Arriving at a large and lavishly embellished *colombage* building topped with a witch's hat, I said I was not that impressed and had seen much grander *châteaux*. At that, a figure appeared in the doorway to explain it was not the main house, but in fact just a *\*pigeonnier*. He was a big chap and holding a hefty hoe, so I decided to go into Lost Tourist mode.

This involves looking anguished or irritated and speaking very loudly and slowly in English while holding any maps or brochures upside down. The ruse works with most minor officials but should not be tried on members of the *Gendarmerie*. I have found ignorance of the law and their language only makes them unhappier and the penalties more severe.

In this case, my theatricals were unnecessary. Putting down the hoe, the man introduced himself and apologised for startling us. He also said he was sorry the big house was closed for repairs, but he would be pleased to show us around the grounds. He hoped we would agree they were like a typical English garden.

I do not have many friends with gardens comprising a few hectares of manicured lawns dotted with painstakingly topiaried shrubs, acres of flower beds, fountains, a maze and a huge lake, but I knew what he meant.

When we had completed the tour he walked us to the gate, wished us well and said he looked forward to seeing us again. When I thanked him and congratulated him on his work and asked if it was not a lot of work for him to keep it all looking so nice, he smiled and said he did have the assistance of some other gardeners.

It was only when we were in the car that my wife asked rather dryly if I had not noticed that the name of the gardener was the same as the one under the coat of arms on the gates.

*\*Pigeonniers or columbiers of varying size and design are found all over France. Like many things, they were introduced by the Romans, who called them columbarium. No stately home or castle would be without one, and they served a number of purposes. The size and elaborate design would denote the power and wealth of the owner, and as well as meat for the table, the pigeon droppings were a valuable fertiliser for the fields. Only owners of a significant amount of land were allowed to have pigeonniers, and their size and grandness had to be strictly in proportion to their wealth and importance.*

*Nowadays, they are a prized possession by middle-class*

*Britons as holiday homes rather than repositories for pigeon poo.*

## Le Perche

We have crossed an unmarked border and entered another historic division of the Orne.

Le Perche is designated as a regional park, and occupies the south-easterly corner of the department. It is said to be a fine example of a variety of French landscapes, with rolling hills and valleys frequented by small streams, fields, forests and the occasional marshland.

Apart from growing cider apples and pears, dairy farming is a major activity, and the world-renowned Percheron heavy horse gets its name from this small corner of the Orne.

## L'Aigle

This small but interesting town is believed to have earned its unusual name because an eagle's nest was found during the building of the castle. Another notable event occurred when a meteorite burst above the town in 1803. Today, the big occasion is the staging of a travelling fair.

Nowadays, travelling fairs are almost unknown in Britain. Children and young people prefer to sit at home playing games or communing with people sitting at home in another place. But travelling shows, fairs and circuses are still big in rural France. The *foire itinérate* at L'Aigle is a long-standing and traditional event which will draw fun-seekers from miles around. Being a traditional French fair, Health and Safety regulations will not apply.

When we arrive we find a large-bellied policeman is the sole representative of law and order. He is sitting in his car, ignoring people who are ignoring any official or sane parking restrictions and concentrating on enjoying a complimentary *gaufre*. These are popular items at all travelling fairs, and are what we would call waffles. Perhaps that is where the slang expression came from, as it is very hard to talk sensibly with a mouthful of waffle.

Basically, a *gaufre* is a leavened batter slab sprinkled with sugar and then topped with a sauce of the buyer's choice. The big policeman has obviously opted for the complete range of flavours, and is happily unconcerned about the rainbow stain spreading across his shirt front.

All around us, happily terrified children are swung up and down, back and forward and round and round in carriages and chairs with no visible harnesses or restraints. Others try to win a prize by shooting at dinner plates with what look like real shotguns, and the lads try to impress the clusters of local girls on the test-your-strength machine. It is interesting that we cannot see any slot machines which involve no more involvement than putting a coin in the slot. The attractions all involve some form of activity or skill level, and my wife points out a typical French paradox at the Dodgems arena. In Britain, the drivers would be intent on crashing into each other's cars, blocking others in and generally causing mayhem. Here they are all carefully avoiding contact and driving in a considerate and restrained manner. As Donella comments, the point about a Dodgems ride is that you drive entirely differently than you would while on the road.

We enter a deliciously aromatic row of stalls selling savoury treats, sweets, ice creams and doughnuts as well as the French equivalent of a hot dog. This is a very spicy sausage of North African origin in a cut-down baguette, with the optional dressing of a very un-French hot sauce. The same boys who were trying to impress the girls with their strength are now showing off by submerging their sausages in the fiery *harissa* paste.

My wife disappears to raid the nougat stall and I try and outdo the local bobby with how many sweet sauces I can load on to my *gaufre*, then we find a bench and watch the action.

Things are warming up as evening approaches, and lights flash hypnotically, sirens wail and people shriek with mock terror. Awful French music booms from a dozen huge loudspeakers, and stallholders compete with the noise as they entice passers-by to try their skill, luck or nerve. It is pandemonium, but a stimulating and innocent way to spend an evening in a small town. Unusually for any mass gathering, everyone is having a good time.

As we leave, I nod to the policeman who has left his car and moved on to the stall for a *merguez* hot dog in a full-size baguette. Sauce squirts out of one end as he bites into the other. He looks at me and his shirt and laughs, but I think his wife will not be happy with his contribution to the week's laundry.

## Mortagne-aux-Perche, Le Theil, Bellême

Heading towards the southern border we take in a trio of small but interestingly different towns.

Mortagne-aux-Perche, a solidly attractive dwelling place on a hill with an impressive 12th-century gateway entrance and pleasing variety of medieval streets and homes. It is market day, and while there we pick up a good ten inches of the local specialty. The town claims to be the black pudding capital of all France and they reckon to sell around three miles of *boudin noir* at the annual festival. Naturally, there is an inevitable fan club whose name translates roughly as the Knights of the Brotherhood of Pudding-Tasting.

We move on another half an hour to the southern border of Orne and the town of Le Theil. This is another place distinguished by the celebrated towns it is near or on the way to, one of which includes our next destination.

An obviously ancient town, Bellême is a very touristy and sporty place. There is a pleasing gatehouse and moat, a church with a 10th-century crypt, some remains of the original ramparts, and a fine collection of sundials. Built on the crest of a natural bowl, the town boasts its own lido, a golf course and popular moto-cross circuit. Another claim to fame is the annual international mushroom festival.

## Haras du Pins

It has been a long day, but on the way back to base camp we stop off at the place Napoleon III was heading for when he called in on Camembert.

Normandy prides itself on its involvement with equine matters, and Haras du Pins is definitely the oldest and reputedly the most striking and aristocratic stud in France.

Founded by Louis XIV, it is known as the 'equestrian Versailles' and with some justification, as the architect of the royal stud buildings were designed by the man responsible for creating the stables at the great palace. It is certainly a very grand place for a horse-breeding centre, and the administrators make the most of it. The estate covers a staggering 2000 lushly landscaped acres, and visitors can tour the stables, harness rooms and forge, and see various crafts being pursued.

From an almost unbelievably grand place for horses to live, we head back to our small tent in a municipal campsite. But as my wife says, although there would be virtually unlimited manure for the garden of the finest quality if we lived in a place like Haras, the window cleaning bill alone would not bear thinking about.

# Boudin Noir flambé

## sur un lit de pommes

This grand-sounding Norman favourite starter could hardly be simpler to make and looks very seductive when served in the traditional way. It also brings together the marriage made in food Heaven of pork and apple. In some parts of Normandy they like to eat the blood almost straight from the pig in jelly form, but we prefer it with oatmeal and other healthy and tasty additives. It is possible to make your own black pudding if you have a source of pig's blood and intestines for the casing, but we find it easier and a lot less messy to buy it.

## Ingredients

A suitable length of *boudin noir* or black pudding
A couple of firm-fleshed, slightly sharp apples. (If you can get them, Reinettes are the officially approved variety).
30g butter
A liqueur glass of Calvados
A tablespoon of cooking oil
A pinch of cinnamon
Some salt and butter

## Method

Peel and core the apples and cut into slices of about 5mm thick.
Melt the butter in a frying pan, and, when hot, add the apples.
Turn the slices from time to time with a wooden spatula until they are a golden brown, then sprinkle with cinnamon, salt and pepper.
Brush the pudding with a little oil, pricking the skin. Grill the slices on both sides under a medium heat.
Drain the pudding on to kitchen paper and then arrange on top of the apples in a flameproof casserole.

Return to the heat.
Just before serving, pour the Calvados over and set alight.

*NB: We think this dish tastes even better if you fry some onions in the gloop remaining when you have taken the apples and pudding out of the pan, but this sort of indulgence is not generally approved of in strictly traditional Norman households.*

*We usually accompany this dish with pommes vapeur, or, to you and me, steamed potatoes. The recipe appears later in this book.*

*Finally, it is compulsory to drink only ice-cold dry cider with this dish, and it must be taken in proper china mugs or stone cups which have been chilled in the fridge. Believe me, it makes all the difference.*

# Pays d'Alençon

Our last day in the Orne, and we shall be sorry to move on. We will also be sad to say goodbye to Serge, Joss the parrot and the friends we have made here. In a strange way I shall even miss my daily battle with the Turkish toilet.

At these times, I think how we spend our lives touching or colliding with those of strangers before moving on. Some will become distant friends; most we will never see again. Irrationally, I feel guilty about losing touch with many of those tens of thousands of people who have briefly become part of our lives. It is frustrating to know that we will never get to know how their lives unfold.

We may never see Serge and Joss and our friends from Jersey again, and almost certainly not the traveller whose tiny tent appeared alongside ours during the night. He is a driven man, except he has no car or motorised transport. To say he is travelling light would not be accurate as it is hard to see his touring bicycle beneath the tiers of baggage and vital accessories. We offered him coffee before he went on his way, but he said he was behind schedule and had some way to go that day.

While finishing his packing, he explained he was about half way through his 4,000 mile personal Tour de France, and every moment was vital. He was sixty, so time, like the days, was growing short. The marathon pedal was a present to himself, and planned when he had found out that his wife had been sleeping with his best friend. He had divorced her, taken early retirement and immediately set out on his journey. Although he did not say so, I got the impression the idea was to put the maximum distance physically and mentally between himself and his former wife, and to spend all his money on the mammoth trip rather than the settlement. If he made it, his journey would take him to every department in mainland France, and if he and the money lasted, he said he would move on to foreign outposts like Corsica, Martinique and even French Guiana.

We watched him pedal away and I said it would be nice to

know how his journey went. But my wife is right when she said our Christmas card list would bankrupt us in a single year if we tried to keep in touch with all the fleeting friends we have made and lost while travelling the roads of France.

~

To some French estate agents I have encountered, a forest can be any wooded area with more than two trees. But the Forêt d'Ecouves is a proper job, covering 58 square miles. It lies to the north of Alençon and was the scene of what is described as a significant tank battle in the August of 1944.

Today it is a popular place for recreational activities; alive with walkers, mountain-bikers and wildlife, but an American tank and memorial sitting at a crossroads is a sombre reminder of the madness and cost of war.

## Alençon

Although it is not one of Normandy's best-known stops on the tourist trail, Orne's leading town has plenty on offer to visitors and residents.

The Hotel de Ville is suitably grand, and nearby looms the ancient Castle of the Dukes. It still serves as a prison, though I believe the dungeons are no longer used. Both of these edifices are perfect examples of buildings made to last and to impress or subjugate.

Alençon also has some fine parks gathering around the Sarthe river, and a museum of fine arts to show off the lace work for which the town is famous throughout the world.

Then there is a wonderfully Gothic basilica, showing its English influence of design as a result of being occupied for a long spell in the Hundred Years War. Surrounded by trendy cafés and department stores, the *Halle au Blé* is a solid but not stolid round Victorian building, built as a marketplace and now an exhibition centre. The tourist office is set in a perfectly preserved townhouse of the 15th century, and Alençon was the birthplace of a recent saint, who we will meet later.

On the downside, the town has the usual stockade ring of ugliness in the form of commercial buildings and parks and tower blocks. The centre also has its share of examples of the poverty of imagination of designers and architects who think that to be different is sufficient justification for an eyesore. Ironically, it was the French who gave us *avant garde*, and proved that a building, sculpture, painting or fashion trend is not admirable just because it is new and unusual.

What makes these baubles suffer in comparison with the fine designs of the past is that Alençon was mostly spared the destruction wreaked upon so many other Norman towns after the D-Day Landings. It was in fact the first town to be liberated by French troops. To us, the giant bowling ball spinning in a fountain and two huge splayed cylinders which look like gasometers after an earthquake do not enhance the streetscene.

Another not-always pleasant reminder of how things have changed in France came with our visit to MacDonald's. It is not that we were in search of a Happy Meal, but to use the free wi-fi.

The restaurant was almost eerily quiet when we arrived, but with noon came the customers, descending on this branch of France's most popular fast-food chain like a flock of starving starlings. Cars screeched to a stop and disgorged small but plump children and sometimes very large adults. As we leave, I make way for a woman who is taller than me in her platform shoes, and would certainly weigh more than me in no more than her thong. She is wearing shorts which are under severe strain, and her sleeveless, cropped tee-shirt reveals a moon of a pallid belly and great slab-like arms covered with tattoos. She has several bits of metal through holes in her nose and ears, and her hair is a virulent shade of purple. I exchange greetings to check if she is British, but sadly she is French. She is not alone, and a number of the young mums share her taste in fashion and body mutilation. This would not be abnormal in any High street in Britain, but we are not used to such cutting-edge Style of the People in provincial France.

Outside, we hurry past tables where fond mothers are force-feeding their children with chips and burgers, pausing only to keep themselves topped up.

I hope I am not a snob and like burgers and kebabs as part of my often unbalanced diet. It is just that we have been travelling in France for more than a generation, and not all the changes seem to be for the better.

## Neuville

As the subject of the previous *French Impressions*, we traced the River Dordogne on its journey from its source half way up the side of a dead volcano in the Massif Central to where it escapes into the sea near Bordeaux. Its meandering marathon of coming up for 500 kilometres makes it one of the longest and impressive waterways in France.

At a little over a hundred miles, the Orne is one of the shortest. In total it travels only through the department named for it and its northern neighbour Calvados before mingling with the waters of the English Channel at Ouistreham, the port of Caen.

The setting for the source of the Orne is also a little more prosaic than that of the Dordogne. There is some dispute as to where it first appears, but officially the Orne starts life in or around the commune of Aunou-sur-Orne, to the north of Alençon. We could not find it, but caught up with the nascent river as it wound past the abandoned *mairie* in the tiny village of Neuville pres Sées.

Despite being within hearing range of what is a busy road for Normandy, the village has a really out-of-the-way and timeless feel. It is the site of a lovely old church and a working farm made up of the grandest of grand buildings. Neuville is also the site of one of the saddest cemeteries we have visited.

Although the ratio is changing, more than two-thirds of French people prefer their bodies to be buried rather than burned at the end of their lives. The British figures are the other way around. Another difference is that in France, cemeteries and burial plots are usually kept in better condition and paid much more attention than people's cars. In the immaculate churchyards and out-of-town cemeteries you will find rows of pristine memorials in gleaming marble, often with a photograph of the deceased on the gravestone. On the day of *Toussaint* (All Saints) all cemeteries come alive with candles and seas of chrysanthemums as families visit their dear departed.

In the churchyard here, many of the older burial places are forlornly neglected, topped with broken and rusting ironwork cages and once-ornate crosses. Those in the saddest condition bear notices that they have been declared as abandoned, and are being taken in hand by the commune.

Most poignant of all are the children's graves. Many of the boys and girls who lay here were taken in their adolescence, like Jean Deschamps, who left the world in his eleventh year. It is sad to think he did not have his share of life.

A gate squeaks and we turn to where an elderly man is entering the churchyard with some difficulty. He is using a stick and carrying a large bouquet of flowers. We watch as he navigates his way haltingly to a beautifully-maintained but clearly not recent grave, on the headstone of which is a photograph of a smiling and beautiful young woman. The old man stops and kneels with a painful effort, laying the flowers gently down on the marble surface.

He senses us watching him, looks across and smiles. Then he looks at my wife and back to me, smiles the sad smile again and then begins to arrange the flowers he has brought. Although no words have been spoken and it is probably my fancy, I feel he is telling me that I should make the most of my marriage and my wife, as, like his, our union will not last forever.

I nod, blow my nose noisily, then leave the churchyard to the old man and his memories. On this lovely, endless summer's day, it is sobering to be reminded of how soon all things must pass.

# CALVADOS

It is difficult to pinpoint what's not to like about Calvados.

Overall, it seems to me that Calvados is a place where nature and history and tradition have all been made the most of, and it feels like a pretty good place in which to live nowadays.

Historically, there is almost a glut of great castles and other grand buildings and monuments, and many have a resonance for visitors from Britain.

William the Conqueror was born in Calvados and his invasion plans hatched and fleet constructed here. And the story of how he came and conquered and made us what we are is told in the tapestry at Bayeux.

In living memory, the greatest armada the world will ever see brought British and Allied troops to the shores of Calvados to fight on and win the beaches and beyond.

Further along the coast from the D-Day beaches are the iconic resorts which were the playground of the rich and idle in the years between the wars. Inland is an eye-pleasingly variety of crags, hills and valleys, sweet winding rivers and the vast central cereal-growing prairies dotted with villages which sing of the past.

Anywhere in the department is near enough to savour the harvest of the sea, and the richness of the land can be tasted in so many ways. There is said to be an ancient law insisting that every dish must be served with cream, and I am not so sure it is a joke. For my money, the best cheeses in the country are found in Calvados, and anyone who says a *café-calva* is not the perfect nightcap (or wake-up tonic) has no sense of taste or occasion.

Whichever way you look at it, Calvados has just about everything the visitor or resident could want. Some would argue that the weather is not always as they would like it, but then those who seek the sun above scenery, culture, history and great food and drink would probably be better suited with the attractions and weather found in Benidorm.

~

Having eulogised about one of our favourite French departments, we find we have arrived in Calvados during a spell of prolonged wet weather.

This gave me the excuse to propose we keep the tent in its wrapper and spend a week under a proper roof, and my wife was easy to persuade. We rarely pay to stay in other people's homes in France as we have so many friends here, but it will be good to have a soft bed. Hopefully, the place we have chosen will not be fitted with a trendy stand-and-deliver toilet.

Because it is a convenient base for exploring the west of the department, and also because it is such a pretty town in such a pretty area, we have chosen to take a gîte near Thury-Harcourt and the *Suisse Normande*.

Our temporary home will be a hamlet near the village of Cintheaux. Even for rural France it is a tiny habitation, and if a couple of families moved away it would literally decimate the population.

# Cintheaux

Cintheaux is home to a couple of hundred people and a strange mix of ancient and relatively modern. In the aptly-named Operation Totalize, the village was virtually wiped out in the process of destroying the 12th SS Panzer tank division. Miraculously, the 12th-century church survived, and is now an official French Historic Monument.

The bombardment means that nearly all the houses in the village are of post-1944 vintage and we are booked into a bungalow near the church.

We are shown round by the bustling and businesslike but amiable Madame Agnes Samson, who is shadowed by a man who is either her partner or the handyman, or perhaps both. Joel comes straight from central casting as a Norman countryman, with a weather-beaten face, an even more weather-beaten Bob Dylan denim cap, and a moustache of which a hirsute walrus would be proud.

The *maison de plain-pied* ticks all our boxes, and has an ultra-modern kitchen and a wet-room bathroom with a big enough shower cubicle to hold a small tea dance in. The toilet appears to be bog standard.

The facilities include wi-fi and a slim-line TV, which is in sleek contrast to the traditional nature of the furniture. Seeing me weighing-up the solid post-war buffet, table and chairs in the dining area, a troubled look passes across Madame's face. When I say how much I admire the furniture, she looks for a moment as if she is about to cry with relief.

Our taste, it appears, is not in line with younger British visitors, who want either very modern or very old furniture. It is not that she does not wish to spend the money to upgrade the furniture, but that it belonged to her mother. The old lady moved here when the family farm became too challenging, and took her favourite furniture with her. All the while it is there, Madame Samson believes her mother is still there.

I say that the atmosphere in the bungalow is so amicable that I believe her mother must still be there, and we will do our best to get to know her.

With this, the lady's eyes moisten again, and she dispatches Joel to fetch a bottle of home-made *calva* so we can seal the deal when money has changed hands.

~

We have been exploring the village, which did not take long. The Samson family plot is in a corner of the churchyard, and we see that Madame's brother as well as her mother lie there.

Next to the church is a grand building which once would have been part of the church but it is now in private hands. As we pass, the great gate opens and a small man with a tiny dog on a lead emerges. He looks like he has stepped out of the past or is on his way to take part in a TV drama about a country village in England between the wars. He is of middle age, with hair sleekly oiled back and a parting so rigidly straight that it looks painful. He wears a hacking jacket and an open necked shirt with a cravat, twill trousers and brown brogues. He looks completely out of place in rural France, so I comment on how historic the church is and ask him if he knows the date of construction. His response assures me he is not British, so I have an intriguing mystery to solve before we leave. If the man is not going to a film set or a theme fancy-dress party or murder weekend, why is he dressed like a minor country squire in the Home Counties?

Along the road, we find another curiosity. Although traffic is rare, the cars, tractors and vans which come through the village towards the main road to Caen drive as usual as if pursued by demons. There are no speed limit signs on the thoroughfare, but as we enter a narrow lane leading to a cornfield, we see a sign warning that a draconian limit of 30 kilometres applies to this short road to nowhere. One of the houses in the huddle is immaculately maintained and has obviously undergone much improvement. The mystery is solved when we see from a small plaque on the gate that this is the home of the mayor.

# Falaise

The giant figure sits astride a theatrically rearing horse, holding a spear aloft in a pose worthy of a statue of a working-class hero in Soviet Russia. It is there to remind us we are in Falaise, the birthplace of William the Conqueror.

William The Bastard - as he was known before it would have been very unwise to use that sobriquet in his hearing - was the son of a Duke of Normandy and a local tanner's daughter. Dad was known as Robert The Magnificent or Robert The Devil depending on your allegiances and again, presumably, whether or not he was around.

A direct descendant of Viking raiders, William was born in the castle in 1028. He became Duke of Normandy at a very tender age when his father died suddenly, and it proved not to be a good career move to become the boy's protector. A series of guardians met sticky ends, but William survived to take his leading place in British history. Given his upbringing and the daily risk of death as a youngster, I suppose it is not surprising he was not known for his compassion and indulgence to those weaker than himself. Had it been in print in those days, it is not likely he would have been a reader of *The Guardian*.

~

Before visiting the castle we take a stroll around the surrounding streets to check out the town.

Falaise gets its name from the giant crag or inland cliff on which the castle sits, and the village would have grown around the fortress, with people arriving and setting up shop to serve the needs of those inside. This tradition of living off the castle has obviously continued into modern times, with shops and bars and restaurants catering for the thousands of visitors who come to see the birthplace and early home of the great man.

Like so many others, the town was mostly destroyed in the bombing which was part of a battle to which it gave its name. The Battle of the Falaise Gap (or Pocket) took place between the 12th and 21st of August 1944 and was the decisive engagement of the Battle for Normandy.

There are more than 800 religious buildings in Calvados, and are or were several places of worship of interest at Falaise. The Church of the Holy Trinity is an imposing building in the shadow of the castle and survived the wartime bombing almost intact. The stained glass windows were destroyed, and were never replaced. The lofty arched ceiling is clad in wood, a feature unique to the Falaise area, and a paint job on the west wall in 1820 hides an unusual fresco. It depicted the solemn execution in 1386 when a pig was sentenced to die for killing a child. There is no record if the sow was buried in a convicted felon's grave, or eaten.

~

The French have been known to go a tad over-the-top with the way they present their ancient monuments to visitors. Here at Falaise is a fine example of how the use of state-of-the-art technology can be unobtrusive in bringing the past alive.

Dotted around the grounds of the castle are posts topped with binocular-type viewers which give a 3D representation of what any particular spot would have looked like when William was in charge.

The reception area is dominated by a giant bust of the Conqueror, which makes him look even more bellicose than the statue in the square. The sculpture depicts him as having a strong-featured face and a soup-strainer moustache which would rival the luxuriant growth sported by Madame Samson's handy man. Contemporary reports indicate that William was, at 5ft 10 inches, tall for his time, with a strong frame and rasping voice. He wears a fiercely angry and suspicious expression and does not look as if he would suffer fools gladly. I do not know how accurately the face is reproduced, but you can imagine how being surrounded by a host of local and foreign lords and barons who would love to unseat you could lead to a certain sourness and distrust of human nature.

Moving on to the reception desk, we are back into futuristic mode. We are given electronic tablets which, when pointed at marked points around the castle, do the same job as the binoculars. The picture changes as the holder moves the tablet, and also relays printed and audio information. Like spacemen exploring an alien world, we shuffle up winding stone stairways and through galleries and high-roofed halls, oohing and ahhing as an empty stone room becomes an 11th-century bedchamber.

Most surprising for we temporary time-travellers is how similar the furniture and furnishings were all those centuries before. Peasants may have slept on straw with their animals, but royalty relaxed on canopied beds with huge square pillows which look like something from a modern-day TV programme about keeping up with the latest domestic trends. Shutters at the windows keep out the winter cold, and in one corner is the medieval equivalent of a fitted wardrobe.

Even more thought-provoking and slightly spooky is the way the long-dead speak to us. The Plantagenets have gathered at Falaise for a family Christmas, and thanks to the latest advances in image-projection techniques, members of the family and key figures appear phantom-like to talk of their lives, successes, failures and deaths. After we hear from Richard the Lionheart, his brother John and their mother Eleanor of Aquitaine, a ghostly seneschal appears to explain and list the vast quantities of capons, geese, eels, trout, salmon and even caviar that will be consumed during the festivities.

We leave as the spectral Richard begins his endless mulling over his gains and losses and painful death. It has been a fascinating visit, and one much enhanced by the chance to meet and hear from the people who shaped our world.

~

We take the scenic route home, travelling north–west towards Thury-Harcourt and the Calvados version of the *Suisse Normande*.

One moment we are squeezing down narrow lanes and avoiding hikers, tractors and deer, the next we are in the Yorkshire Dales. The landscape opens up and in the distance smoke curls lazily up from the chimney of a pink cottage. I do not know if it is true but have been told by locals that in the old days, pig's blood was added to the lime wash mix to make it water-resistant. Whether or not this is so, it makes a pleasant supplement to the colours of summer.

Now we are travelling downhill through a thickly-wooded area. The road is overhung with a tunnel roof of branches and through the gloom I see a man struggling towards us, accompanied by a pony. As we get closer, I see that it is in fact a very small man with a very big dog. The ill-proportioned pair pause and look at us with disinterest as we pass then continue their climb. I am about to comment when my wife pre-empts me by saying she does not know why the little man does not climb aboard the giant lurcher and ride in comfort.

All at once we break free and out into a great valley, the sun sparkling off the waters of a stream. Alongside the road is a collection of caravans, but not the sort normally seen traversing any holiday route. There are no cars or vans in the field, but a dozen large horses are tethered to a line between two metal posts. The caravans they pull are of traditional design, like covered wagons with wood where the canvas would be. They are painted in the brightest of colours, and nearby a group of gypsies sit round a fire on which a blackened old pot is bubbling. As we pass, I see they are weaving baskets. It is somehow good to know that some of their race still choose to spend their travelling lives behind a horse rather than in a white van, and make things for tourists to buy rather than collect scrap iron and mess up driveways.

~

At a supermarket in Thury-Harcourt we encounter a special offer unlikely to be staged in our local Tesco in Hampshire.

On a great, glittering heap of ice in the fresh fish department rests what looks like a smaller version of the central character in *Jaws*. The giant mouth gapes open to reveal the rows of jagged teeth, but rather than the cold expression of a natural killer, the shark looks mildly surprised to find himself in his current location. The creature must be ten feet long from nose to tail and from the dorsal fin back, the body has been sliced into swiss-roll like portions. A gaggle of housewives has gathered around the display and they are discussing how exactly the flesh should be cooked and what it should be served with. A poster by the display announces a really special cut price offer per kilo of fresh *requin*, but the Norman ladies seem in no hurry to buy.

We watch as a white coated, hatted and gumbooted assistant uses a marker pen to reduce the price. When I ask him how low it will drop, he shrugs and looks at his watch. It is only an hour to closing time, he says, and if they don't sell it soon there will be a lot of fish to throw away. The local cats will be ecstatic, but not his boss.

*I checked out the unfamiliar name on the poster when we got home, and found that 'requin' is indeed the word the French use for shark. The article also said the origin of the name was disputed. Some authorities claim it comes from the Latin requiem, but a far more satisfying explanation is that the name comes from the verb 'reschignier', which means 'to grimace while baring teeth.'*

The nice lady on the TV *météo* bulletin has assured us there is a less than zero chance of rain. She confidently predicts widespread sun and little wind, so we have decided to stay close to home and explore the locality by bicycle.

Accordingly, we flex knees, pump up tyres, fill thermos flasks, pack haversacks and oil our chains. I think about oiling my bottom in accordance with old bicycling lore that this somehow helps ease the pain of a long ride, but my wife says it is bad enough having to wash my underpants anyway, and she will throw them away if I make the task worse.

It is remarkable how even a modest ride in the countryside can become a small adventure, especially when it is in another country. You see so much more than from a car, and being on a bike makes you feel somehow more part of your surroundings. If you are on a bog standard bike you may even feel almost as if you are a local. Another bonus is that a lengthy bicycle ride also works up a major thirst and justifies the quenching of it.

We have studied the local maps and decided to head due east from Cintheaux, so pedal past the church and take an old road bridge across the busy N158.

Leaving the roar, smell and smoke behind, we enter a different world. Another aspect of cycle riding in the countryside is that you become so much more aware of the contrasts between busy highways and deserted byways.

Our way leads through a vast and obviously fertile plain, sitting contentedly beneath an upturned bowl of blue. On one side is a golden carpet of wheat, and on the other looks like a giant's allotment. The rich soil has yielded acres of what look like peas, and further on, row after row of beetroots stretch into infinity. Birds sing and the odd cotton-wool cloud scuds across the sun, the terrain is flat, the surface of the lane is good and the wind is at our backs. In short, we are in cycling Heaven. Best of all, in an hour of pedaling we have yet to even see a car.

Unless you have done a bit of rural cycling, you can have no idea of the intrusion a motor vehicle can make or the fear it brings. In town, you expect passing traffic and perversely, the busier the route, the slower drivers are forced to go so the safer you feel. In the countryside, an occasional encounter with a speeding vehicle is much more noticeable and feels much more dangerous.

No matter how thoughtful and careful the driver, half a ton or more of metal roaring by a yard or less away from your fragile bundle of flesh and bone is always underpants-threatening. I find the terror increases exponentially with the overtaking speed, but even at 30 mph the experience can rupture your commune with nature and turn your knees to jelly as your heart rate surges and your breathing shortens and Fear Wobble threatens.

I cycle an average of fifty miles a week, and drive four hundred. I know how infuriating smug, self-righteous or completely self-centred cyclists can be, but I also know how almost unbelievably careless, cavalier and life-threatening some drivers can be when they feel they are being held up or inconvenienced by someone on a bike. I am sure they are not intending to maim, kill or even frighten the pants off you, but that can be the result. I think it is more an inability to see themselves or their loved ones in your position than malice, but dangerous driving habits show how thoughtless and self-obsessed so many people can be. If I were in charge, as well as making beer a medicine and therefore available on prescription, I would pass a law requiring all motorists to spend a month on a bicycle.

But we remain unmolested as St. Sylvain hoves into view, and gather speed as the lane begins to run sharply downhill. We are relieved of the obligation to pedal, but in cycling terms this is not always a good thing. Whichever route you intend coming back on, going downhill on a bicycle is a bit like Life. At some time you know you will have to pay for the easy bits.

## St Sylvain

At last count, 1,374 people called St Sylvain home, which makes it the second most populous town in the canton.

Regardless of the statistics, the residents do not seem to be fond of the idea of dropping in to their local for a drink and a chat. Although there are two bakeries, at least one hairdressing salon and even a DIY store in the main street, the only bar has long since ceased to trade. But while admiring the unusually-designed church, I see those locals in search of stimulating entertainment have evidently not got too far to travel. Apart from an upcoming flea market and senior citizen dinner, the notice board announces that the band Skip and Die will shortly be performing in the *salle de fetes,* and that their repertoire includes those old favourites *Love Jihad* and *Death Samba.*

There is a trendy-looking restaurant near the crossroads, so I park and go into the cool, dark bar. Fragrant odours and the sound of clashing pans issue from the kitchen, and two bow-tied staff members lurk in the shadows. Although there are no customers, it looks as if they are expecting a busy lunchtime. The barman is friendly enough in manner, but looks relieved when I order coffee and then escort my Desert Storm shorts and string vest out on to the terrace.

My wife is studying the menu and reports that the set meals range from 25 to 40 Euros a head. There is a special of the day, but we decide to eat later and elsewhere. The food may be excellent here, but price is not always a guide to quality. Sometimes, it can mean the opposite.

Our coffee arrives and is priced at almost twice the going rate in a rural bar. But it is very good, served in trendy and obviously expensive cups, and there is the bonus of a courtesy chocolate-covered hazel nut.

St Sylvain is clearly a bit of a through-town, and lorries, tractors, vans and cars continually lurch around the roundabout and past the terrace.

A half hour has passed and still there are no customers but us. It may be that they are late eaters round here, or perhaps the establishment does its main business in the evenings. It looks as if the owners know what they are doing, but there are always other, unpredictable factors at work when you try and persuade people to come and eat with you. The rate for restaurants failing in France is even higher than in Britain.

Suddenly the church opposite announces noon. The clanging goes on after a dozen strikes, and shows no sign of abating as we drink up and get back into the saddle. The strident noise pursues us down the road and out of town, and I wonder if the bell ringers are having an elongated session, or if the incessant pealing is a recording which has stuck. Or even if the verger is getting his revenge on the restaurant after what he saw as an overly pricey meal.

## Couvicourt

The bells of St Sylvain are quickly left behind and we enter another placid sea of cereal. This is serious growing country, and not a weed, buttercup or other wild flower is allowed to get in the way of maximising the harvest.

Then as I try and work out how many zillions beetroot salads could be made from the ocean we are passing, the quietude is shattered and we hear a great flapping and cawing and screeching. Directly above us a buzzard is being harried by two crows, and the struggle seems like two Hobbits attacking an Orc.

Although it is at least twice their size and looks far more menacing, the buzzard is obviously getting the worse of the encounter. After a final frantic screech and flail of talons, it flies up and away, leaving the crows crowing in triumph. The practice is known as 'mobbing' and crows are better at it than virtually any other species. They routinely attack flying predators much more powerful than themselves, and are protecting their young and their territory along with their air space.

I wave admiringly as they preen themselves on a telephone wire. We like crows as they are one of the most intelligent species of wild birds. They mate for life and pool their knowledge when food is about rather than try to keep it to themselves. They have more than twenty calls, and I can do one quite well. I have no idea what it means but I try it out on them as we pass by. They ignore me, so perhaps French crows, like humans, speak a different language.

The going gets a little harder as we leave the plain and head back towards the N158. We can see sunlight glittering from the roofs of cars but the road is still too far away for us to hear even a hum.

It is the sacred time of the *midi*, but even if the entire

population of the village/hamlet of Couvicourt is at lunch, it is somehow quieter than quiet. Like the abandoned village in the *Suisse Normande*, there are no cars either moving or parked, and not a sound of life apart from the chickens scratching in someone's front garden. The street is lined with neat gardens and vegetable plots, but all is deadly still. It is like a scene from one of those films when mankind has been wiped out by a deadly cosmic radiation burst or plague.

We pause at the pleasingly named Fork and Baguette restaurant, but it is closed and the owners presumably eating on their own behind closed doors, or at someone else's establishment.

~

The road becomes ever noisier as we pass a sign towards Caen and what is rather aptly called *Le Dénouement* of 1944.

Heading westward and away from the Route National, Donella points out what looks like a medieval siege engine in the middle of a field of corn. It is a massive structure of wooden beams with a platform at the top and is at least 40 feet high. At first I think it must be the tallest shooting tower in France, then see a rusty silo hidden behind it. We look up at it and think how it could not have been much fun carrying a heavy sack of grain up the dozens of steps to the top of the giant storage container.

We leave the plain and it is pleasant to pass fences and hedges and small fields of buttercups and grass being nuzzled by groups of giant Charolais beef cattle. I avoid their eyes as I know what I am planning to eat for lunch.

After another climb through a sun-dappled stretch of woodland pasture, it is downhill all the way to our next stop.

# Bretteville-sur-Laize

Bretteville–sur-Laize has only a marginally larger population than St Sylvain, but the residents seem to be keener on eating and drinking or just going down the pub.

The town supports four bars and restaurants and a betting shop with a bar, and there's a pharmacy, a bank, butchery, bakery and even a cinema where there is a weekly showing of a popular movie. Whatever the secret of success is for a village-sized French town, this place has it. It may be how the facilities and car park cluster together in the centre or that through-traffic is diverted to a tour of the outskirts. Whatever it is and how much those factors contribute to the general ambience, there is a bustling but quietly contented air about Bretteville-sur-Laize. In our experience, this feel is the X factor common to all thriving mini-towns.

Dismounting, we look at menu boards and find that the owners of the bar and restaurant opposite the car park seem to have hit on a winning combination and formula for their lunchtime offering. There's a mixture of very traditional Norman dishes, or a choice of pasta or pizza or even hamburgers.

Hungry from our exertions, we start with the paradoxically named *plat d'Anglais* of assorted French cured and smoked meats and sausage, then I shelve my plans for a steak in favour of the lunchtime special.

My wife chooses a crackling crème brulée for pudding, while I work my way through a selection of Calvados' finest cheese. Our meal is accompanied with a complimentary bottle of rough red wine after an appetiser of very dry and very cold farm cider served in stone and stone-cold cups. To finish, we linger over a brace of *café calvas*. The main dish of braised ox-cheeks was exactly right after our exertions, and the cider, wine and apple brandy more than eased the saddle soreness in my own cheeks.

~

A sombre and thoughtful end to our day, and I feel somehow guilty to have lived so long and done so much while in the company of men who did not have the chance to grow old.

Although less than a quarter of a mile from the busy road to Caen and as with most places like this, there is a solemn silence enclosing the Canadian War cemetery on the outskirts of our village.

In common with war cemeteries across the region, this one is kept in completely immaculate condition. The 2099 bone-white headstones stretch in perfect symmetry across a sward where not a weed is permitted to show its face, and the flower beds surrounding the central monument are clearly under constant supervision and care.

There is a register containing the name and age of all those lying here, and I see that most were in their early twenties. The youngest is a Private Clarence Earnshaw of the 5th Battalion, the Black Watch Royal Highlander Regiment of Canada. He gave his life and all that it may have held for another country almost 72 years ago on the 14th of August 1944, and was just 17.

There is also a visitors' book, and it is filled with messages of relatives who have come to see their fathers and grandfathers, uncles and great uncles. Many entries finish with simple but very poignant messages.

As we leave, we pass two elderly ladies. They are walking slowly along the row of headstones nearest to the gate, stopping to lay a single wild flower on each grave. They would have been very young women when the D-Day landings and battles took place, and I ask them if they intend to pay tribute to every fallen soldier. They both smile as if the answer to my question should be obvious, and one says that these young men gave their lives for France and freedom, so a single flower seems not much in return.

# Joues de Boeuf avec pommes de terre en purée

When living in an old water mill in Normandy, we rented out our fields to a neighbouring farmer, who happened to be the mayor. My first act when meeting *Monsieur le Maire* was to refuse any rent, and to give him lifelong grazing rights.

He would not accept this obvious act of bribery in return for future favours, so we settled for an annual slap-up dinner at his farmhouse. Jean's wife Solange had no near-rival when cooking traditional dishes at the wood-burning stove, and over our years at the Mill of the Flea we must have eaten our way through at least one of the Le Chevalier herd from tongue to tail.

Our first memorable meal centred on this simple but superb dish of cow-cheek with creamy mashed potatoes:

## Ingredients

A kilo of beef cheeks (you may have to shop around!)
One large and roughly diced onion
A carrot, also roughly diced
A stick of celery, ditto
3 large and finely chopped garlic cloves
Some fresh or dried thyme (several stalks or a couple of teaspoons-worth)
Three bay leaves
A cup of good beef stock
Two cups of a substantial red wine (like Merlot)
Some seasoning and olive oil

## Method

Prepare the beef cheeks by removing any large, fatty membranes, then dry off and season each side.
Put a small amount of olive oil into a heavy pan or casserole dish and sear the cheeks over a high heat until nicely browned.
Remove the cheeks and keep warm.

Turn down the heat, and add the garlic, onion and carrots. Sauté for a few minutes and then add the celery.

Pour the wine into the casserole dish, scrape the brown bits off the bottom of the pan then add the cheeks to the casserole.

Add the rest of the ingredients and cook in the oven on a medium heat for around three hours, turning the cheeks once.

Put the cheeks aside and remove any thyme stems and the bay leaves.

Use a hand blender to make the braising liquid into a smooth sauce.

Bring the sauce to a simmer over the heat and reduce to a nice, thickly rich consistency.

Remove from the heat, return the cheeks to the sauce and keep warm.

For the puréed potatoes

Put a kilo of floury potatoes (still in their skins) in a pot, cover with water and add some salt.

Bring to the boil and then simmer until they are very tender.

Meanwhile, put a cup of milk into another saucepan and add a clove of garlic, a bay leaf and a sprig of thyme.

Bring to the boil, then take off the heat and leave to infuse for around ten minutes.

Remove and discard the garlic and herbs.

When the potatoes are ready, peel them while hot, then put them through a food *mill/ricer set at the finest setting and into a pot.

Beat in the butter a piece at a time, then bring the milk to the boil again and beat it in.

*In case you are not familiar with the items, a food ricer is a handle with a container at one end and a plunger which forces the cooked potato or other vegetables through holes in the bottom. A food mill is a Heath-Robinson-looking device like a tapered saucepan without a bottom. It has a crank handle which pushes soft or cooked foods through a disk which has suitable *hole sizes for the job in hand. Lacking either of these kitchen gadgets, you can use a hand blender or even a fork if you have the energy and patience.*

Another fine morning.

We will need to stock up on groceries as France will be closed until Tuesday.

Today is a public holiday and when it falls on a Friday, many people will take Monday off as well. When the holiday falls on a Monday, it is the custom to warm-up by taking the preceding Friday off. The practice is called 'the bridge' as it stretches and spans the weekend.

There are eight public holidays in England and Wales, though Northern Ireland also takes time off to celebrate St Patrick's Day and the Battle of the Boyne. Scotland also has St Andrew's day. Though it seems much more if you intend going shopping or get any official business done, the French have less than a dozen official days off. These include Victory in Europe Day, Ascension Day, Bastille Day, Assumption Day, All Saints Day and Armistice Day. What makes it appear that the French have a lot of time off work is the frequency of strikes and demonstrations. *Manifestations* are a national sport, and taken in good part by all French people, even when they are inconvenienced by wildcat stoppages.

## Thury-Harcourt

To many Normans, Thury-Harcourt is the jewel in the crown that is the *Suisse Normande*. Depending on which way you look at it, Thury is at the start or the finish or somewhere along the route on the Calvados side of the border, and very much geared to visitors.

Sitting on a fast-flowing, bendy stretch of the Orne, the town is a popular venue for campers, caravaners, gîte-stayers, water sportists, bikers and hikers. It is connected by a Green Way to Caen, fifteen miles to the north. We are here to test out the ride, and for me to see if my freshly-oiled bottom will cure my Saddle Chafe.

Apart from the newly-laid all-weather surface and the promised views and serenity, the particular attraction for me is that the trail is almost flat all the way, yet surrounded by the undulations of the *Suisse Normande*. Most people will not know this, so I will be able to impress them by casually dropping in to the conversation that I have cycled a good bit of the Norman equivalent of Switzerland.

Once upon a time the town was known just as Thury, but sponsorship from the Duke of Harcourt at the start of the 18th century made the addition seem a good idea. It is yet another place which suffered in the battle for Normandy, and nearly three-quarters of Thury was destroyed. But it does not feel like a reconstructed town, and is a generally friendly, humming and sometimes even jolly place.

Before starting our ride, we are to stoke up our energy levels by having lunch with a helpful lady who works at the tourist office. She it was who found us our accommodation at Madame Samson's bungalow, so we have asked her out to lunch and left the venue to her. I am hoping this is a wise idea.

~

A pleasant hour in good company, but also an expensive reminder of how people will pay so much for so little if it is fashionable.

As we had done the inviting, I had suggested a MacDonald's when discussing venues. My wife had not bothered to reply, and had asked our guest if there was somewhere serving traditional Norman dishes. Consequently, we arrived at an innocent-looking establishment on the outskirts of the town.

The warning bells rang when a very thin man with a bow-tie slid silkily across the vast expanse of slate floor and asked if we had a reservation. Worse, he asked as if we would be beaten up and thrown out if we had dared to cross the threshold without prior agreement. This is always a key indicator of price, as the owners are sending out signals that:

a) the place is so popular that you need to book.
b) therefore the food must be really good.
c) logic dictates that you must expect to pay for this level of quality and reputation.

As it was nearly an hour into the lunch period and there were just six customers spread around ten tables and forty chairs, I wanted to ask if there was a coach party expected, but a look from my wife warned me not to start a fight.

I had expected to be seated near the window to make the place look busy, but the waiter led us to a dark corner as if he did not want passers-by to look in, see me and assume I was a typical customer.

He swept off as if glad to get away and I took stock of our surroundings. Decor and theme can tell you a lot about a restaurant. Cheap and good places invariably have a lived-in and often shabby look. This is because the premises are always busy and the proprietors do not have to bother trying to impress their customers. Over-priced and pretentious eateries used to be all dark wood, an abundance of soft furnishings and gilt mirrors and snow-white damask tablecloths with napkins shaped like water-lilies or swans. Nowadays, the interior of the most up-themselves premises usually look like a modern art gallery, or as if the bailiffs have been in and removed most of the fixtures and furnishings.

This one has gone for the art gallery style, which is very suitable when you think how modern art is all about gullible and snobby people paying breathtaking amounts for daubs and 'installations' that anyone could have knocked up in minutes.

Everywhere is black from the floor to the table tops and walls and even ceiling. This is not to hide the dirt but to impress on the punters how creative and *avant-garde* the owners and therefore the chef is. The walls are lined with small monochrome paintings with no frames which presume to have great depth and meaning. They also insinuate you are a philistine if you do not get what they are saying. The paintings each bear price tags so that you may have a takeaway, and I walk across to look at one just to get the owner/waiter excited. I see it is priced at about what a dirty weekend in Paris would cost, but to be fair I suppose it is only in keeping with the price levels on the large blackboard menu. Using classic snob-appeal, rather than whisper the outrageous cost of a plate of cow guts or bottle of fizzy water, the establishment is shouting them.

I pretend I am not hungry after a big breakfast, and settle for the special dish of the day. It is obviously special because of the price. The ladies order and I look gloomily around while we wait for our drinks. I have ordered *kir as an apéritif, and scored a small victory by ordering the traditional Norman appetite-whetter with cider rather than Champagne. It is not much of a victory, as the three glasses cost more than a bottle of reasonable bubbly from the supermarket across the road.

Nearby, there is the unmistakable sound of middle-class Britons at lunch in France. I hope I am not classist, but I find people who think they are better than me because of the accident of birth or the benefit of an expensive education profoundly irritating. It is much more irritating when these people live in or claim to live in our capital city. The foursome opposite are not actually braying, but talking loudly enough so I will end up knowing where their children went to school and go to university, where they live in London and how big and splendid if demanding their holiday property is. They will not say how much their home in Islington is worth as that would be vulgar, but they will know I will know just how privileged and wealthy they are. For my money, Oscar Wilde got it right when he talked of people who know the price of everything but the value of nothing, but perhaps I am just jealous of their fine lives and the freedom money can bring.

Predictably, the Brits have chosen fish and chips from the blackboard menu. They have done this to demonstrate that they are veterans of French cuisine and find it amusing to eat a British dish while abroad – as long as onlookers recognise the ironic gesture. It will also enable them to tell the owner how much better his fish and chips are than anywhere in Britain, and what a pity it is he cannot cross the Channel and show them how it should be done.

I eavesdrop some more, and think about pointing out that they are paying five times the price they would have paid even in an Islington chippie - if there is one - but that would have been breaking the rules. They have to make sure we can hear their vaporous babble, and I have to pretend not to hear it.

They know we are British because our guest wanted to practice her English, which is why they are saying what they are, and saying it loud enough for us to hear. I have already tried switching to French, but they immediately did the same to show they could.

*Kir is a popular apéritif which dates back to at least the 19th century but was popularised by a Burgundian mayor of that name after the Second World War when the former hero of the Resistance served it to visiting overseas delegations. Officially, it consists of white wine with a dash of crème de cassis (alcoholic blackcurrant juice), but variations include using peach juice (Kir Pêche) or Champagne instead of white wine which makes it a Kir Royale. Normans have made it their own by using cider with the cassis, making it a Kir Normande. If a spot of Calvados is added to a Kir Normand, it becomes a Cidre Royal.*

~

Like the bill at the pretentious restaurant, the setting is almost breathtaking.

By that I do not mean that it is at all exotic or on a grand scale, or that there are waterfalls or snowy-peaked mountains in the vista. It is just a perfect place to be in on a sunny summer's day in rural France.

The French look after cyclists very well, especially off-road. Once, this was a railway line cutting through the heart of the *Suisse Normande*. The trains no longer run, but the line has been left in place as a reminder of the past. Most importantly, the way alongside the old track is wide and beautifully constructed and finished to provide a perfect cycling, running, walking or even skating surface. Veteran off-road cyclists, we are used to gravel, pit-stones, or sometimes the luxury of a well-tamped and smooth composite surface. But ahead of us stretches mile after mile of gently cambered tarmac which will never become worn and damaged by motorised traffic.

A further commendable touch is that interference with nature has been kept to a minimum. There are few signs except for distance markers, and only the occasional well-chosen site for benches and tables. The one at which we are sitting is on a bridge across an ox-bow in the Orne, which sparkles and gurgles and sings by with no other competition to overcome but birdsong and the whirr of pedals.

Another most pleasing aspect is the low level of lycra louts. Cycling as a competitive sport is an obsession here, and many men and some women like to ape their heroes. Regardless of their shape, they wear figure-hugging costumes, and mandatory accessories include swept-back and menacing dark glasses, which must be worn regardless of whether or not the sun is shining. There is also a competition to see who can wear the silliest-looking pointy helmet. As well as looking intimidating, the lycra lout likes to put other cyclists in their place by whizzing by very close and with no warning, face set in grim determination as he strives to beat a personal best time.

We have seen hardly any of the species so far, and this is because, perversely, they prefer busy roads to country tracks. This is not because of any suicidal tendency, but the busier the road, the more people will see them. Vanity is very much the name of the game for this type of look-at-me *cycliste*.

As we prepare to leave, a man pulls up who makes my combination of Desert Storm shorts and aged airtex vest and Mickey Mouse ball cap look restrained. He is wearing lycra tights but with gumboots, what looks like a genuine World War II leather flying jacket and a motor cycle crash helmet and goggles. His sit-up-and-beg bicycle looks as if it is being held together with rust, and on the crossbar is strapped a child's seat. On it is sitting a small dog, which looks perfectly content.

My wife knows I will not be able to resist striking up a conversation with this interesting person, so gets up and walks across to the parapet of the bridge to look at an old and derelict mill sitting on the opposite bank. I begin to stand to greet the man, but slide forwards off the seat at his feet. As he helps me up, he asks me conspiratorially if I have oiled my arse. I give him a warning look, as my wife is not aware that this morning I decided to try out the alleged remedy for saddle-chafing on a long ride. Having to use materials to hand, I have found that constant pressure has forced the goose-fat through even the closely-woven material of my shorts and I am finding it increasingly difficult to stay in the saddle or anywhere else I choose to sit.

~

We are well on our way to Caen and have stopped at the intriguingly-named Bridge of Brie. There is a picturesque-looking auberge on the far side of the river at a junction on a country lane, and it is busy with fellow Green Way users and motorists, taking a break to enjoy the sylvan surroundings.

Some are having a late picnic, and once again I admire how well the French do outdoor eating. Not for them a shop-bought sandwich while sitting in the car. They will have cars with boots the volume of a particularly capacious Tardis, from which the male will produce and erect tables, chairs, parasols and in extreme cases a whole kitchen range. Even some of the cyclists come well prepared, and a couple are taking their ease on the river bank in collapsible chairs on either side of a low table. On it is a whole roast chicken and bowl of salad, two plates and some cutlery, a cruet set and a bottle of white wine in a cooler. I am disappointed not to see a candelabrum.

At first I think they must have carried all this equipment in their capacious rucksacks, but then see that one of the bikes has a trailer attached to it. It is of the type usually used to tow small children or pet dogs, but in this case obviously carried all the makings for a moveable feast.

~

It is an interesting statistic that the average person passes wind fourteen times a day, which amounts to around half a litre of gases a day.

Perhaps surprisingly, 99 percent of those gases are odourless. The noxious smell of the other one percent is caused by sulphurous emissions. Many of the foods which cause the most flatulence are good for you. Despite their protests, women are as likely to break wind as men. Finally, some farts have been clocked at ten feet per minute on exit.

I only mention these fascinating facts because a French cyclist who caught up with my wife after our break asked if I was jet-propelled. Thinking she had misunderstood the woman's French, my wife said that my bike was not battery-powered. To this, the woman responded in perfect English that she was referring to my persistent breaking of wind for the three kilometres she had been following me.

~

We pass through a canyon of soaring stone and then a thickly wooded forest, then out into a clearing where the long, straight stretch of railway line is polished from constant use.

Towards us clanks what looks like a bench seat on wheels. It is running on the rails. Two adults sit side-by-side at the front of the contraption. They are pedaling furiously, while three children sitting behind urge them on to greater effort.

As the *vélorail* lurches by, we take our hats off and wave to the family as if sending friends off on a long rail journey.

Around a bend and high above the opposite bank we see a magnificent house perched on a giant crag. Two people sit on the balcony, secure and snug in their eyrie. It is too far away to know if they are looking at us, and there is no response when I wave.

More dwellings come into view as we near the outskirts of Caen, and we stop to look at the sort of property that holiday home-hunting Britons say they would die or even kill for. It is a two-storey railway worker's cottage with a steeply pitched roof of red tiles. It is guarded at the front by a neatly-kept paling fence enclosing a small garden. The back is actually, as the French say, *surplomb* over the river, sitting on a goalpost of stone pillars which rise from the bank. The door-like first-floor window is bolted back against the brickwork, and from it hangs a duvet. The country tradition of airing the bedding in this way completes a picture for any postcard. Some day, I think as we continue our journey, it would be nice to settle in a place just like this.

~

The contrast could not be more complete. Twenty minutes ago, we were cycling through silent and sylvan surroundings alongside a river and past solitary buildings. Now we stand in Lower Normandy's major town, where giant cubes form canyons through which rivers of traffic flow.

More contrast as we leave the post-bombardment modernist outskirts and arrive at the town centre. The grandest town hall I have seen is obviously the venue for some sort of noteworthy event, and an immaculately turned-out *gendarme* is guarding the ornate entrance. He is wearing his official-function *kepi,* and springing to attention and saluting guests as they step from gleaming black limousines.

An even grander limousine pulls up and the policeman goes into overdrive. He steps forward and manages to open the door, bow and salute at the same time. From the car steps a diminutive figure in a suit. He scuttles on short legs to the entrance, where a row of dignitaries are lined up to receive him, and I realise that there is something familiar in his gait.

I leave my bike with my wife and slip my backpack off as I walk across the terrace, fumbling inside for my camera as I duck under a line of tape stretched between two traffic cones. Before I have made a dozen paces towards the entrance, the doors of a black car with smoked windows open and four young and fit-looking men scramble out. They have close-cropped hair, and look as if they are more used to wearing uniforms than black, close-fitting suits. They surround me, and one slips his hand inside his jacket. I note he does not remove it until I show my camera and explain I was only hoping for a selfie with the President of the Fifth Republic.

Time to move on and we have taken an almost tearful leave from Madame Samson and her live-in gardener.

Photographs have been taken and e-mail addresses, promises to keep in touch and small gifts exchanged. Agnes has given Donella an elegant box of chocolates, and I have presented our hosts with one of my books. Neither speaks much English so I do not know what they will make of it. But they seem pleased and insist I sign the copy.

As I am getting in the car, Madame Agnes gives me an awkward hug and asks if I think an echo of her mother still lives in the house. I nod and say I am sure of it, and I believe it is part of the reason we have felt so welcome there.

With a hoot and a wave and a scrunching of gravel we drive away from people and surroundings we have become so familiar with in such a short time, yet will probably never see again. It is a curious thought to think of all those lives and daily routines and small worlds into which we have trespassed and which will carry on without us as if we had never passed that way. There is a view that other people and places only exist when you are there, and vanish like Brigadoon when we leave them. I can see the argument, but think it based more on vanity than logic.

## Blangy-le-Château

It has not been an untroubled start to our stay.

The town of Blangy-le-Château looks as if it were made to have a picture of itself put on a chocolate box lid if the French did that sort of thing. The mobile home disguised as a wooden cabin sits, as promised, beside a babbling stream a short walk from the village and with views across a water meadow to the ancient church. It all looks very promising, but we have squatters.

We have been paying for use of the cabin since this morning, but were asked by the owner to delay arrival as the previous occupants needed until one o'clock to vacate the premises.

After a long, hot drive, we arrived to find a woman lounging in a decided manner on the raised terrace. She was wearing what my wife later explained were very expensive denim jeans and a floral blouse knotted under where her breasts would have been had she not been thinner than the wooden cladding on the former caravan. When I explained we were the new tenants, she looked at me as if I had not paid the fee for speaking to her, and said they needed more time for her husband to pack properly and for them to leave the place as they found it. I followed the irritatingly fashionable man back to the car park and it was hardly a surprise to see their gleaming car bore Paris license plates.

In the way that much of the rest of the UK can take or leave Londoners, it is hard to find a French person with a good word to say about Parisians. Their arrogance, rudeness and snobbery offends even their fellow countrymen, and that is saying something when you think how good all the French can be at arrogance, rudeness and snobbery. Over the years I have asked the owners of bars, restaurants and hotels as to who they prefer as customers, and even drunken English booze-cruisers come above Parisians.

I overtake the man on his return to the cabin, and without asking, decide to help with the moving of the designer baggage and the lady on the terrace.

~

A couple of hours later and we have taken possession of our home for the next week. The Parisians have left in a huff, and clearly did not think much of my energetic assistance with moving out. But I have shown them that a Briton with right of occupation is not to be trifled with.

The cabin is attractive and very reasonably priced in rental terms, and comes complete with TV, sound system and all manner of power gadgets.

Our problem at the moment is that we can't make use of any of them. Five minutes after the squatters left, the light in the fridge blinked and died in common with all other electrical appliances.

We have found the welcome booklet and followed the clear and detailed instructions for ensuring the switch in the cupboard is on and all the fuses in place, but cannot make the kettle work, the water cylinder heat up or the TV and lights to come on.

The real problem is that we cannot ask for help at the office, as being a public holiday there is nobody on duty. We cannot ask the owner as, because the bar is shut, there is no Wi-Fi facility with which to send an e-mail. Getting a man in is beyond question as, even if we could find an electrician working today, his call-out rate and charge for work done would be more than we are paying for the week's rental of the cabin.

As dusk falls we return from a consoling drink in the local *bar-tabac and* hear English voices coming from a radio inside one of the nearby mobile homes. The owner has a friendly face and manner, and explains the caravan has been his holiday home for a dozen years.

He obviously knows his way around the electrical set-up and comes to the cabin to check that we have got all the right buttons pressed and switches on. It seems we have, and we are about to give up, lock up and go back to the pub when he has a sudden thought. Have we, he asks as if only an idiot would not have done so, checked that the mains power lead is plugged in?

We follow him to where a heavy-duty cable emerges from the cabin and runs under the raised terrace and into a clump of trees. We pick up and follow the cable through the gathering gloom like potholers using a guide rope to retrace their steps, then find the answer to the mystery. The plug at the end of the power cable to our cabin has been pulled out of its rightful home in a socket in a box attached to a tree.

As they could hardly have thought we would not be needing or using any power during our stay, the departing tenants must have decided to vent their spite by disconnecting the power and teaching the English invaders it does not pay to tangle with a native of Paris, let alone a pair of them.

## Pont L'Évêque

For me, a tourist-friendly Norman town does not really live up to its job description without a river running through it.

Luckily most conform to this romantic fancy and Pont l'Évêque seems to play host to at least a couple of rivers and also a canal.

Any town which bears the name of an iconic French cheese has to have a head start, and Pont l'Évêque has some stunning buildings in the old quarter and a truly striking town hall. It also boasts a host of enticing pavement cafés and an excellent *pâtisserie* with a window display of elegant and intricate pastry sculptures which literally look far too good to eat.

On the downside, the town suffers from a noisy and dangerous through-road, which is made all the more offensive by proximity to the ancient buildings and bridges it funnels thunderous traffic through. As we walk along the narrowest of pavements in search of the tourist office, the wing mirror of a monstrous camper brushes my elbow as it lurches by, leading me to examine the rapidly-sprouting bruise as I think how this of all towns deserves a by-pass, and no price would be too high to make it so.

~

For some reason, the town which gave its name to one of the country's most celebrated cheeses appears not to bother to even make mention of the connection.

Most French towns with the most tenuous of links with a celebrated personage or product will make sure you know about it. Some will try for brownie points on the basis of being the birthplace of someone who knew the wife of someone whose name has gone down in history. But here it is almost like they want to keep the cheese connection quiet. There are no giant replicas of the distinctive square boxes on any of the roundabouts on the outskirts, and so far we have seen no plaques, monuments or statues commemorating anyone connected to the invention or development of the deliciously sharp cheese. Other places are not so modest. In Vimoutiers, for example, there is even a statue of a cow of the sort which produces the milk from which comes Camembert.

At the art gallery-style *pâtisserie*, the owner raises an elegant eyebrow and even looks dubious at the very idea of a museum to cheese. Nobody we ask in the street knows of any commemorative features, and we cannot ask at the tourist office as, being a public holiday, it is of course closed.

Next to the entrance, however, is a board with light bulbs illuminating the most noteworthy attractions in and around the town. We press buttons and find that there are five distilleries and one *cidrerie*, but only one cheese producer. It does not say if he makes the brand that the town gave its name to, only that the premises are on an industrial estate outside the town.

But we are pleased to see that the authorities have not forgotten or neglected to pay tribute to other historic connections. Next to the notice board is what looks like a half-scale model of a hybrid between a Hurricane and Spitfire fighter plane in flight. Beyond that is a large bed with an obviously recent and impressive floral display. The sea of multi-coloured flowers and plants is broken with hand-written messages from old and young townspeople to the Allied troops who laid down their lives for the freedom of Pont l'Évêque, Normandy and all France.

*NB. We did return to Pont l'Évêque on a day when the tourist office was open, and came away with armfuls of brochures and lots of first-hand information from the nice lady there. She told us that the canal from the town was an important route for goods in transit to and from the River Seine, and the town first came to the attention of the English when we burnt it during the Hundred Years War. The knights and squires of nearby Noyon were not happy about this act of early booze-cruise tourist vandalism, especially as the town lost several of what they called handsome hotels. The enraged Frenchmen chased after the English and slew hundreds. Fifteen prisoners were then taken back to the town and beheaded so townspeople could see justice done. A good few centuries on and more than half the town was destroyed during the battle for Normandy.*

*Nowadays the population is around 4000, making it a small town for its apparent size if that makes sense. As to the much-feted cheese, wc learned that Pont l'Evêque dates back to the 12th century and is said to be the oldest French cheese in production. First created by Cistercian monks at an abbey near Caen, it is a 'raw' uncooked and unpressed cow's milk cheese with an orange rind and a soft centre. It is generally ranked alongside Brie, Camembert and Roquefort in popularity, which gives it a high rating indeed.*

*It is also said to have an odour reminiscent of the Norman countryside. Some aromatists say it smells slightly mouldy or of a typical barn. It seems a strange way to praise a cheese, but I think I know what the claimants mean.*

# Vache Chaude avec Cidre

This is a bit of a cheat if you believe cooking traditions and recipes should be sacrosanct. *Chèvre Chaud* is a popular starter, and as the name ('warm goat') implies, is usually made using goat's milk cheese. However, we have tried the dish made with Pont l'Évêque, and found the distinct flavour and creamy texture did the job more than admirably. Sometimes this sort of salad is served with just the toasted cheese, baguette slices and oiled lettuce leaves, but we know a couple of very popular restaurants which like to go for the full monty as described here:

## Ingredients

Some non-crinkly lettuce leaves
200g Pont l'Évêque cheese (rind removed)
12 x one-inch slices of baguette
A spring onion
Some mustard
Some good olive oil
A tablespoon of wine vinegar
Seasoning
2 dozen *lardons
A clove of garlic
Some toasted walnut pieces
A bottle of very dry cider
The yolk of an egg (**optional)

## Method

Fry the lardons in only a little hot oil so they will crisp up.
Rub one surface of the bread with garlic.
Cut and mould the cheese to fit on top of the bread rings so the cheese is a centimetre or so high.
Sprinkle pepper on top of the cheese and put the rounds under

a grill.

Mix some oil and vinegar with a ratio of 3-1, adding a bit of mustard and a dash of cider and some pepper and salt to make a sharp but smooth vinaigrette.

Rub the oil on to one side of enough lettuce leaves to line a pudding bowl.

Put the lardons and toasted cheese baguette rounds into the bowl and mix with some pieces of oiled lettuce leaf.

Sprinkle the walnut pieces and finely chopped spring onion over the dish.

Dribble a little cider lightly over the dish and drink the rest.

*Lardons are the nearest the French come to bacon, and are small cubes of unsmoked fatty pork which has been cured with salt. They are used widely in French cooking to add flavour, and may be threaded into meat joints which are to be roasted or braised. This process is known as, wait for it, larding.

** I believe the practice of serving the yolk of an egg in half a shell with the salad may be peculiar to Normandy. The customer chooses whether or not to use it, and if so will tip it on top of the salad and give it a good stir - or not.

As noted before, Upper Normandy seems to me to have more of an up-market image than the lower half. This may not be so, but it does seem to get a bit swankier the more one travels eastwards towards the border. Mind you, Lower Normandy can justly claim to have some of the best beaches.

Today we are going to work our way along the golden strip which was the premier playground of the rich and idle of both sides of the Channel, and where the bars, restaurants and casinos were a favoured haunt of brigades of chinless Bertie Wooster look-and-sound-alikes.

~

It is yet early in the day, but we have already encountered a rabid Hornblower.

The incident happened as we passed through the pretty town of Beuzeville. It is market day and the centre was busy with traders setting up their stalls. Because they are paying for their pitches, they are understandably taking even more leeway with the local parking regulations. Vans are slewed across the road, with the magic flashing hazard lights excusing the most crazy and inconsiderate excesses. Crates of vegetables and fruit litter the way, and I lost sight of the road momentarily as a large sheet of wrapping paper was wafted up from the gutter and performed its function by wrapping itself around our windscreen.

As I threaded slowly through the obstacle course, the rearview mirror was filled with the front of a large, battered and very dirty van. I could see the driver's bellicose face, which was as purple as an over-ripe aubergine. One hand was flying up and away from the wheel in the classic gesture of exasperation, and the other was hammering away on the horn. As it honked incessantly, the van came even closer as if trying to shepherd us through the marketplace like an irate collie, with sharp barks replaced by the angry squawking of the horn.

I do not think this new fashion for informing drivers in front that they are not going fast enough to suit the person behind will catch on in Britain, as much bloodshed would result. I believe that French and other Continental drivers are so much more aggressive partly because they know it is unlikely physical violence will ensue.

The inevitable result of the horn-blowing is to cause me to slow down, which I have found is the best way of making the pursuing driver even more unhappy. I also like to accompany the slowing-down with a casual and amicable wave, as if I have mistaken the aggressive hooting as a friendly greeting. This is guaranteed to make my pursuer even unhappier.

The beeping and the bumper-to-bumper harrying continued until we were well clear of the town, when the driver suddenly jammed on his brakes, made a five-point turn in the narrow lane and scorched off back towards Beuzeville. While the vehicle was broadside on, the lettering on the side of the van identified the driver as a purveyor of quality root vegetables. Thinking about it, he was probably attending the market and had become so incensed by my refusal to speed up that he had pursued us for miles beyond his destination just to vent his spleen. If there is a God, Monsieur Aubergine would have returned to find his space taken and nowhere to sell his wares.

~

The second Hornblower of the day and it is barely noon.

Having travelled the distance to the moon and back by road in rural France we are used to being held up by tractors, especially as harvest time approaches. But this must be the first time in a quarter of a century that we have held a tractor up. It was certainly the first time one hooted at us to get a move on.

My wife thinks she has the answer as to why we are coming in for the honking treatment, and it is not that I am slowing down or driving more cautiously as the years pass. She believes it is simply the make and model and origin of the car we are driving. Until recently, we had a four-wheel-drive monster with French license plates. It looked a bit off-putting because it was never cleaned in the five years we owned it, and the number of dents and missing parts ensured other drivers avoided even parking in the next bay. Like a dog with one ear, it looked always ready for battle. Regardless of how I drove it, the scarred and battered veteran of the road silently dared drivers to get right up close and personal. It was a challenge which was rarely accepted, but things have changed dramatically now we drive a small, new, virulently turquoise and very shiny Citroën Picasso.

The very pristine-ness of the bodywork seems to make drivers want to despoil it. More important are the preconceptions and conclusions made by other road users. My wife thinks we are now treated differently on the road because we are seen as an older couple with a safe little car and, despite the evidence, are driving more timidly than we need. Perception, she rightly says, is all.

For myself, I just miss the days when I was in charge of the battered behemoth and inviting all comers to have a go if they thought their car was hard enough.

## Honfleur

We know we are nearing the coast as the twin giant wishbone structures of the *Pont de Normandie* appears above the horizon.

The deceptively slender-looking bridge spans the Seine, links Le Havre to Honfleur, and was hailed as a triumph of *avant-garde* design and engineering when it was opened in 1995. At the time it was the longest cable-stayed bridge in the world, and held the record for the longest distance between piers of its type.

It is a slightly painful if nostalgic return for us. In the year work started on the bridge, we came to look at a property for sale at Honfleur. Then, it was a mostly unremarkable fishing port on the southern bank of the estuary with a good name for seafood in a handful of restaurants. The property we had come to see was made up of two near-derelict cottages. They sat on the very edge of the quay, and the asking price was £8,000. For the pair, that is. Unbelievably, the price did not seem a must-buy bargain. In those early days of our small adventuring in France, we were also put off by the prospect of taking on a significant building project in another country.

I still wake at night and think of what we walked away from, but after a tear or two I put things in perspective. We only know what has happened and not what might have happened if we had taken a different course in our lives. And as my wife says, the more you do, the more things you are bound to regret not having done.

~

The grand place we are driving through now must have been parachuted in, some years after our visit to Honfleur. Memory can be unreliable the further away the time and place and event, but it seems to me that it must have been another place where we viewed the derelict quayside cottages.

When we were here last, a handful of fishing boats sat on mud berths in the harbour and we had no trouble getting a seat in one of the bars and eating places nearby. Now the giant marina is awash with gin palaces and shiny yachts that seem to come equipped with lithe young women in small bikinis. Where there were a handful of restaurants, every building facing the quay seems to have been converted to an eating place, probably including the ruined cottages we viewed.

However many restaurants there are lining the waterside, the number of covers is clearly not enough to meet the demand on this glorious summer's day. Every chair on every terrace has a bottom on it, and people are actually queuing. Hordes more are descending on the quay like a crowd streaming towards Wembley on Cup Final Day. It is a sun-kissed Saturday in August, but I have never seen so many people so intent on spending huge amounts of money for something to eat.

Honfleur is undeniably attractive in a picture-postcard way, and has come a long way since its origins as a fishing village and then a commercial port. As trade flourished, wealthy Honfleurais built tall and imposing homes alongside the *Vieux Bassin*. Nowadays, the main trading is of food and drink to those who flock here. Apart from eating and drinking, visitors can wander round the beautiful old timber-framed and slate-clad houses, check out any number of museums, wonder at the giant

17th century salt granaries, or take a look at the largest tropical butterfly house in all France.

We decided to pass on all these attractions and not to join the queue at the restaurants as, being lunch time, the banks will be closed and we will not be able to apply for a loan so we may buy a modest meal.

~

Clear of Honfleur, we enjoy the scenic drive along the *Côte Fleurie* and particularly the way that the towns along this part of the coastline have not become joined up.

On the south coast of England, a visitor would find a continual string of homes and hotels and other commercial outlets along any habitable stretch of coastline. Here on the north coast of France there are still many green gaps between bricks and mortar and each town has retained its individuality. Ten minutes after leaving the heaving crowds and brashness of Honfleur, we are cruising past orchards, fields and old cottages. There are also small and as-yet unexploited villages not a hundred yards from great swathes of sandy beaches.

But there are also places where the *bourgeoisie* of the last century have left their mark on the coastal landscape.

For my money, there are few dwelling-places more curious and curiously appealing than the overblown holiday homes found on the Calvados coast. They exist elsewhere, but here they have been developed into almost an art form. The first rule is obviously the bigger and more bizarre, the better.

Some are the size of hotels, and all are awash with an eyeball-spinning mix of styles and fancies usually associated with English follies. Most will be disproportionally tall, as if to look down snootily on surrounding properties and the bucket-and-spade brigade. The exterior will always be *faux-columbine*, with upright and diagonal and sometimes cubist designs for the planks fixed to the standard custard-yellow and stippled rendering. There will be precariously oversized wooden railed balconies aplenty, and the steep pitch of the roof will mean it often ends in a point rather than a ridge. Sometimes there will be a tiny observation room or turret mounted at the very top, and strange rooms and chambers and features will crop up anywhere on the top floors and appear added on as an afterthought. Another constant feature will be the way the eaves of the roof will extravagantly overhang the walls, supported by giant wooden scrolls.

Overall, the result looks like the interbreeding of the Bates motel in *Psycho*, the Adams family residence, a medieval watchtower and Heidi's Swiss cottage writ large. Mock them as we may however, I and millions more would love to own one.

## Trouville-sur-Mer

We have arrived at Trouville-sur-Mer, and are disappointed to find no Wodehousian characters strolling along the promenade in straw boater and striped blazer.

The permanent population is around five thousand, and there must be that many visitors here today. Being the middle of the two hour lunch break, most of them are, as in Honfleur, taking lunch outside the string of restaurants overlooking the sea. It is a nice day, but many French people like to dine or even take coffee in *plein air* regardless of the weather. This may be because they like to have a smoke with their food and drink, enjoy the views at places like this, or simply enjoy being looked at.

Trouville was popular with such French literary giants as Dumas, Proust and Flaubert, and is said the town was 'discovered' by a young landscape painter in 1825. Charles Mozin took his illustrations of the humble fishing village back to Paris, showed them around and started a trend. Jean-Baptiste-Camille Corot and seascapist Eugene Isabey did some of their best work here, and Monet and Boudin famously painted scenes of 19th-century frock-coated and hoop-skirted members of the Paris *bourgeoisie* strolling along the boardwalk.

At the end of the promenade and overseeing goings-on with a somehow fondly proprietorial air is the hugely domed and glitzy casino. Inside, more than two hundred slot machines lie in wait for those visitors who have not spent all their money in the restaurants. In curious contrast, across the road and housed in an almost as grand a building is a sign of the changing times in the form of a *Monoprix* retail outlet.

Just as we are beginning to enjoy our leisurely sightseeing tour along the prom, a now-familiar sound breaks rudely into our reverie. It is the third Hornblower of the day. Although we are travelling at the same speed as the convoy of cars, the driver behind seems to think we should either veer off the prom and into the sea, or follow his example in harrying the cars in front to get a move on. As if reading my thoughts, there is a sudden frantic outbreak of horn hooting, and every car in the slow-moving cavalcade seem to have joined in. I begin to resemble the aubergine-faced vegetable trader from our encounter this morning, and am about to jam on the brakes and go and discuss with the driver behind how bad manners can be infectious, when I look again in the rearview mirror and see there is an old-fashioned besom broom fixed to the top of his car. There is a lady in a very white outfit beside the driver, and I realise that the hooting was not aimed at me.

Somehow I have inserted myself in a wedding procession, and they are following custom by sounding their horns as they parade through the town. I look at my wife, then try and look like a wedding guest as I reach for our own hooter.

## Deauville

Officially and however unlikely the match may seem, Trouville is twinned with Barnstaple in Devon. In reality it has far more in common with its *doppelganger* resort not a mile away over the bridge across the estuary of La Touques.

Trouville is the slightly older, but Deauville can claim to be amongst the first seaside resorts in the country.

Along with its neighbour (and not a few others), Deauville claims the title of 'Queen of the Norman Beaches' and of being one of the most prestigious seaside resorts in the country. The town goes some way to justifying the claim with its international film festival, swish hotels and marinas and casino to rival its twin across the bridge. Both are the nearest resorts to Paris, which explains the size and grandeur of the buildings, and the discreet odour of money which wafts with the sea breezes along this part of the Flowery Coast.

Deauville is also a bit higher up the ladder than Trouville when it comes to twinning. The countryside surrounding the town and its two racecourses is the main horse breeding area in France and as a result is officially paired with Kentucky and Lexington in the USA and County Kildare in Ireland.

~

Another mile and another spiffing resort and ville-on-sea. We travel through Benerville-sur-Mer, then Blonville-sur-Mer and Villers and Villers-sur-Mer. All have immaculately maintained streets and buildings, floral displays and long, sandy beaches. Despite it being the height of the season, all look as if they have just been prepared for a photo-shoot for a brochure. Here there are none of the discarded cans, bottles or instant barbecue sets you would find on a typical British beach. In general, the French do not do litter, which is why there are so few public bins in popular places. They actually do take their rubbish home with them, or at least the older people do.

Another curious fact is there are no fat or ugly people. I don't know if there is some sort of local by-law forbidding flabby, white people in badly-fitting costumes littering the beach, but it would appear so. We decide to test my wife's theory with a dip, and my baggy bathers and almost luminously white torso excite no more than a few curious looks and a fit of crying from a little boy I smile at in passing. As my wife says, I must remember to take my vest off when exposed to the sun as it has left me looking like I am wearing a white brassiere.

## Cabourg

In Houlgate we hit more prime Gothic-horror holiday villa territory, and right on the promenade is a classic. Other houses have chimneys; this one has an octagonal tower welded to the side as if by afterthought and rising two storeys above the roof.

The Hotel Normandie must be the biggest single building to be completely colombaged, ever.

Approaching Cabourg, we pass the entrance to a Tennis Club and further along, an immaculately kept bowling green. The mostly elderly players are wearing straw hats and whites and rolling rather than throwing the balls. The sign also said Bowling Club rather than *Club-Bowling*. Perhaps it is an English expat enclave, or perhaps the club is staging an English day in the way we like to dress up in striped tops and silly berets and drink lots of indifferent wine on Beaujolais Day. Or it may be that they are perfectly respectable citizens who prefer bowls to *boules*.

On our last visit we pedaled along the prom and were encouraged to do so. The dedicated stretch is another example of how the authorities look after cyclists.

As a resort, Cabourg dates back to the middle of the 19th century, and in the way the coast further west suited the D-Day invasion, the three miles of flat and sandy beach are ideal for a variety of sports or just taking one's ease.

Cabourg first came to attention in 1058 when William was warming up for the invasion of England, and drove the troops of Henri I into the sea here.

Nothing much happened to talk about after that until the middle of the 19th-century, when two Parisian financiers arrived to look at the idea of creating another watering hole for the rich and indolent. By now, the railway had opened up the coast, and by the end of the century, the barren stretch of coast had been transformed.

As with the other resorts, Cabourg was a popular haunt for a number of big guns of literature and art, and was immortalised by Marcel Proust in his massive life's work. *A la Recherche du Temps Perdu* was published in seven parts from 1913 to 1927, and Cabourg becomes Balbec. Now that the magic of e-books allows me to carry a virtual library on my travels, I have no excuse for not reading the series. I make an effort to read at least a page a day, but fear it may take longer for me to plough through than it was to write. As someone said, life is short, Proust is long.

Le Grand Hôtel retained its name in the second tome in *In Search of Lost Time*, and forms the centrepiece of the resort. Proust liked to stay in room 414 and wrote an allegedly mesmerising passage about the view from his window.

On our last visit I got off my bike and climbed the steps to look at the discreet tariff card enclosed in an ornate box by the grand entrance. The prices were also mesmerising, and I took my cap off and put it beside me as I sat on the bottom step to regain my senses. As I shook my head and wondered how even the richest people could bring themselves to spend that much on a bed for the night, a very smartly dressed lady approached the steps stopped beside me and started fiddling in her designer handbag. My wife grabbed my greasy cap and hustled me away before I could discover if the lady was looking for her room key, or for a spot of loose change for the old *vagabond*.

~

Back to our level as we find a friendly-looking PMU bar in the main shopping street.

Outside, people sit enjoying watching the sun or waiting for the results of a bet. My wife crosses the road to inspect the contents of a pricey-looking shoe shop, and I am dispatched to order the drinks.

Inside, the bar is cool and dark, which may be why all members of staff ignore me.

One older lady is inspecting a glass as if the meaning of life may be found inside. Another is standing with her back to the bar, hands behind her back and staring dreamily at a point on the far horizon. The third is leaning on the bar talking earnestly to a young man whose hairstyle makes it look as if his head comes to a point. It may be the latest fashion, or because the crash helmet on the bar indicates he arrived by motor bike.

I am not perturbed and do not take it personally when nobody notices that a customer has arrived at the bar. As in Britain, service levels in bars can vary greatly, and nobody is better than the French at reverse customer service techniques. The women have to spend this lovely day in a boring bar serving mostly old men, so the customers are going to pay in more ways than one.

After a few minutes, the pretty young lady is still talking intimately to the young man with the pointy head, and the dreamer is still staring into space. The woman inspecting the glasses has moved on to the next in a row of at least fifty.

Another minute of trying and obviously failing to look appealing, I move into stage two, which involves clearing my throat noisily, coughing, and finally tapping a coin on the top of the bar.

There is no response, so I skip stages three and four and go for the big finish. Staggering back from the bar, I give vent to a histrionic death rattle, roll my eyes upwards, clutch my throat and fall to the floor.

In most pubs in Britain and depending whether I was a regular, the bar staff would have been shocked, unsurprised, annoyed or perhaps amused at my bad impression of a man expiring through terminal thirst. Here, nobody on the other side of the counter takes any notice. This is also true of the handful of customers, who are concentrating on the closing stages of a buggy race in Paris.

Eventually, I climb to my feet and the glass inspector comes over as if nothing has happened, then raises a quizzical eyebrow.

I order our drinks and tune in to the conversation between three elderly men further along the bar. The race in Paris is over, tickets torn up and thrown on the floor in disgust, and talk has turned to the strange ways and even stranger language of those who live across the border in the region that is part but somehow not part of France.

With an air of authority, one of the men lifts his glass of red wine and explains that in Brittany one would order a *gwyn gwen*, and say *eyrmad* instead of *santé* when toasting a drinking companion.

He looks across and sees that I am listening, so I raise my glass and confirm what he is saying. I go on to tell them the words for 'same again' and 'what's yours' and they take me at my word and drink up.

Outside, I tell my wife about the exchange with the men, and that they had mistaken me for a Breton. It shows, I say, my accent must be good if they thought I came from another part of France. She takes a long pull at her shandy and invites me to consider that their error may have come about because my accent is so bad it is obvious I come from somewhere in the country where French can be a second language.

Our last-but-one day in the cabin and department, and we shall be sad to leave both.

The sun rose majestically over the church as we breakfasted on the terrace overlooking the stream. We had oven-fresh baguettes and croissants from the local bakery, and were joined by a couple of moorhens, a solitary coot and a duck and her brood. They have become regular companions when we eat on the terrace and unsurprisingly look very sleek and well-fed. Although one assumes they are French, they like sliced bread, though prefer Livarot to Cheddar cheese. We are constantly told by do-gooders that bread is not good for birds, but they look well on it and nobody appears to have told them it is an unhealthy diet.

## Lisieux

The former capital of the Pays d'Auge, Lisieux has been a regional centre of power since medieval times.

But its roots go back a lot farther. Writing about the Gallic Wars, Julius Caesar refers to a Celtic town on a hill, and it is this one. That's quite a time for continuous occupation, and may account for the way Lisieux feels so at ease with itself.

It is another town which was the subject of no little dispute during the Hundred Years War, and Thomas Becket took refuge here after he upset Henry II. Until World War II, the town was renowned for the range and splendour of its Renaissance and Gothic buildings.

Nowadays, it is a modern, buzzy and friendly sort of place with a population of 30,000. It is another one of those towns which seems busier and bigger than the sum of its numbers would suggest.

In spite of its modern buzziness and very temporal activities, there is a deeply religious focus to Lisieux. Apart from its day job of sending millions of bills to Norman households, the town is the second-most important pilgrimage destination in France, as it is the resting place of a relatively very recent saint.

Saint Thérèse of Lisieux was the youngest of nine children, born in Alençon in 1873 to a middle-class family in trade. She became a nun at the age of fifteen, joining her two elder sisters in the Carmelite community at Lisieux. Thérèse died of tuberculosis at just 24, and left a collection of writings which included an autobiography entitled *The Story of a Soul.* They were collated and published by her sister Pauline a year after Thérèse's death, with a very limited audience expected for the 2000 copies. Following growing awareness and admiration for her pronouncements on how best to lead a life in God, she was canonised in 1925.

Thérèse is now one of the most popular saints and at the time was the youngest person and one of only three women to be canonised. Her parents were also made saints in 2015.

We toured an exhibition of photographs and her writings at the Carmel, and I was puzzled by the contradiction of her life and works and the events after her death. She was the most modest and self-effacing person who said that she wanted to be unknown, yet wrote her memoirs. People usually do that because they want to be noticed. Because of her writings and their publication against her wishes, she became world-famous and is adored by millions. The Society of the Little Flower is dedicated to spreading devotion to Saint Thérèse, and I was fascinated to see that their website offers a St Thérèse Blog. I clicked on in hope of a miracle, but sadly it was not by her.

## Orbec

Now we really are in what the French call *France profonde.*

In Ancient Norse, 'Orbiquet' is said to mean something like 'stream with plenty of trout in it'. This sounds a good enough reason to set up camp nearby, and the town which L'Orbiquet runs through is now one of our favourites.

Sometimes a town can be less than the sum of its parts, and sometimes more. For us, Orbec falls into the latter category. It also has that magical 'X' factor which, being an 'X' is by definition beyond definition, I suppose.

Any list of features which contribute to the appeal of the little town must include the aforementioned river/stream. Then there is the way the main street is lined with beautiful and beautifully maintained colombage buildings. Some are graced with very handsome herring-bone - patterned brickwork between the timbers, some with rendering. Unusually, the rendering has been painted in the range of pastel hues which would have been popular when the properties were built.

Today is market day, and the colourful frontages make a striking backdrop to the stalls, stands and vans lining the street. Another plus factor is that all traffic is being diverted round the town. We have found that being free of the risk of injury or death while browsing at market much enhances the experience.

Further adding to its appeal, Orbec appears to have no straggling outskirts of modern buildings and commercial outlets. The way we came in, the centre of town is no more than a few hundred yards from its start.

Apart from a very fine up-the-market restaurant (*see the recipe for Calvados soufflé later*), a special attraction for me is that Orbec is one of the few small French towns where you could go on a proper pub-crawl without walking far enough to get out of breath. First on the agenda would be the traditional drinking pub, complete with amiable host, and just up the street is the lunchtime special bar, run by an attractive and personable middle-aged woman. Then comes the touristy bar in plumb centre of the high street, and virtually next door is a very typical and well-run *bar-tabac*.

We opt for the *tabac*, where I cause confusion by ordering a pot of tea and a car. When we have sorted out that I meant *thé au citron* not *thé au Citroën*, we are served by a pleasant proprietor who makes little of my mispronunciation.

As we sit and watch the action in the marketplace, a man who looks as if he could be much younger than his looks suggest arrives on a mobility scooter and parks adroitly at the next table. Before he has properly settled, the lady of the house appears with a glass of beer and some sweetmeats on a saucer. He appears not to be able to reply with more than a nod to her greeting, but Madame puts her tray down, pulls up a chair and begins a one-sided put obviously welcome conversation.

As she helps the man lift and put the glass to his lips, another middle-aged woman with a shopping bag arrives.

Almost absent-mindedly but without causing any risk of embarrassment, she produces a handkerchief, makes a pad on which she spits, then briskly rubs at a mark on the shoulder of the man's coat. She then ensures his collar is not too tight and straightens his tie, pats his chest affectionately and leans over to kiss his cheek before continuing her journey. Not a word has been said, but the tenderness shown by the two women is enough to make me pretend to have caught a fly in my eye.

As my wife says, this is the sort of town which has clearly remained essentially the same for centuries. Obviously, much has changed, but generations of the same families have been born, lived and died here. They will not all get on and newcomers will have arrived, but this has not threatened a bond and general feel of them all being in it together. Despite the ease with which people throw the word about nowadays, 'community' really fits the bill in Orbec

~

It is fair to say that few members of the national *Gendarmerie* would be likely to win a popularity contest. Their comrades in the Civil or Municipal force are attached to towns to deal with everyday matters of law and order and can be on a different footing with the locals.

The officer on foot patrol at Orbec is a big, brawny chap wearing well-tailored and crisp blue shirt and trousers, with his holstered pistol slung low on one hip. He is also wearing a broad smile, and pushing a pram as he does his rounds of the market. The contrast of death-dealing weapon and baby carriage is literally remarkable.

The officer takes his time and is obviously enjoying the occasion, stopping to share a pleasantry with regular stallholders and answer questions from and give directions to strangers. At some stalls he puts the brake on the pram, reaches inside and holds up a baby for inspection and approval. Now and then and I think to remind people he is the boss, he wags an ironic finger at a trader who has taken liberties with the boundaries of his allotted space or committed some other minor transgression.

This Gallic equivalent of PC George Dixon is obviously well-known and even celebrated beyond the town limits. As we watch, a man points at his camera and makes an obvious enquiry. The policeman nods and is joined by the female companion of the cameraman. They strike a pose, and the woman reaches out towards the holstered gun. The policeman assumes a mock-severe expression, and the meaty forefinger goes on wagging duty again. The photograph is taken, then the policeman summons a stallholder to man the camera and take a shot of himself pretending to handcuff the man while the woman looks on in theatrical horror. Rather than demean the man's authority and presence, this easy familiarity seems to increase it.

The policeman continues his rounds and we make ready to continue our journey.

As the streets at the top of the town were so crowded, we took a chance and left our car in a Blue Disque zone without the necessary permit and as we near it, my heart sinks when I see something tucked beneath the windscreen wiper. But then I see it is no more than a pamphlet advertising a get-together in the park the following week. A whole pig is to be roasted and there will be entertainment and a beer stall, and even tastings of local cheeses and, of course, apple brandy. By then we will be in another department, but I hope to return to see Orbec and perhaps pose for a photo with the friendly and welcoming bobby.

~

Though it is made in other Norman departments, Calvados claims the name for a very fine apple brandy.

Elsewhere in France, snobbery might dictate that brandy made from grapes must be better than brandy made from apples, but even die-hard French traditionalists are being won.

When we lived in Lower Normandy, home-made apple brandy was known as *calva* or simply *goutte* (old Norman French for a drop or a taste) and took an active part in everyday life. A glass might be taken with coffee (*café calva*) first thing in the morning or last thing at night; or between courses at dinner as *trou Normand* to 'fill the hole' between meals and re-awaken the appetite. It was used in cooking or as a medicinal aid, and the rougher varieties might come into play to help start tractors on a frosty morning.

It may or may not be related to the enthusiastic consumption of the fiery brew, but I remember reading that Lower Normandy once had the lowest consumption rate of toothbrushes in northern France. This may have been because regular consumers of *goutte* needed no other aid to keep their teeth clean, or had no teeth to brush as a result of over-consumption.

In those not-so-long-gone days, families with their own orchards and a hereditary licence held the right to brew their own supplies. But the mobile distillery would be a regular after-dark visitor to many homes without an official orchard, and sometimes those without a garden. The favoured container for the illicitly-produced version was a lemonade bottle wrapped in a copy of the local newspaper. To try to stem cottage-industry bootlegging activities, there was even a local law which made it an offence to be found with sealed bottles of home-made *calva* in your car. Bizarrely, if there was a part-filled bottle rolling around in the front seat that was fine, as it was obviously not *en route* to an illegal sale but for personal consumption only.

In our time in Normandy we attended many late-night stillage sessions. It is a wonderful experience to see and celebrate the miraculous transformation of juice from your own apples to the tears of Norman angels. We also visited some fascinating *calva* cellars disguised as carpenters' workshops and even pig styes. Today, though, we are going to find out how the professionals do it.

~

At first sight, the site of the start of the brandy-making process at the distillery of Roger Groult at St Cyr du Ronceray is not at all technological.

We are standing in a yard with a rough-cast concrete floor

riven with channels. (Cattle byres have a very similar arrangement to allow the residents' pee to run away). As our friendly guide Evelyn explains, this is the very traditional start of the journey for the mountains of apples dumped in the yard by trusted family farms within a twenty kilometre range of the distillery. Strong jets of water propel the apples along the channels to the next stage, leaving unwanted debris behind.

The apples are then shunted into undercover presses, where the pure juice is extracted. In the eminently satisfactory way that nothing is wasted in the countryside, the *mouet* or apple pulp will be returned to the farms to be fed to the animals. The liquid is now nascent cider, which is piped into storage tanks to await a visit to the distillery area.

Here at the family-run business, the distilling is still done in the traditional way, and the equipment looks exactly as you would hope. Copper tubing gleams and connects giant onion-shaped containers bristling with dials and portholes. Below them, pure oak chips feed the boilers which heat the cider and reduce it to a fraction of its volume.

We move on, and I stand spellbound on the threshold as our guide unlocks the door to where thousands of gallons of young apple brandy sit quietly waiting for maturity and to give pure pleasure to people across Normandy, France and the world.

The arched cellar is lined on either side with large oak barrels known as *fûts*, each of which contains 400 litres. The bungs are removed regularly for breathing, testing and tasting purposes, and the bouquet is literally intoxicating.

When the contents have served their time, they will be moved on to even bigger barrels to spend the years before bottling. These *foudres* can hold 6000 litres.

An hour later, and our journey from apple to liquid gold is complete and we stand in the area where the *dégustation* ceremony takes place.

We have seen the finest of Calvados made, and now we taste it. I still carry fond memories of those days of sampling our and our friends and neighbours' freshly distilled moonshine, but the tasting session here proves that the finest apple brandy in France is worth the time, the cost and a long wait.

# Livarot

On the 17th of July 1944, the mayor of this small town brought first-aid dressings to a wounded Field Marshall Rommel. This year the Tour-de-France passed directly by the town, but those are far from the main claim to fame for Livarot.

On the roundabouts, Brobdingnagian cheese boxes demonstrate that, unlike Pont l'Évêque, the town is loud and proud about its connections with such a famous French cheese.

An otherwise unremarkable place, Livarot is (not always the case with French cheeses) the home of the major producer of the cheese of that name. The Graindorge factory also produces Camembert, Pont l'Évêque and the lesser-known Neufchâtel.

The business began in 1910, when farmer Eugene Graindorge turned his talents to making a living from cheese. As demand increased, he took milk from other producers, and soon Livarot was establishing a reputation nationwide. Nowadays, Graindorge exports to the USA, and the business that started as a one-man show is a very modern and switched-on affair.

Some romantically-minded if naive people are disappointed that a great French cheese is made in bulk in a shiny and sterile factory. In fact, the establishment is a perfect example of using the most modern production and marketing techniques while emphasising the traditional and natural nature of its products.

Outside the building by the visitors car park is an old flatbed lorry of about the same vintage as Grandfather Graindorge. Inside in the reception area there is a display and information area of which any trendy exhibition centre would be proud. Even better, there is an unaccompanied tour which is almost spookily efficient in guiding visitors through long, gleaming, brightly lit and sterile passages which house windows giving a view down into the factory. At the Calvados distillery we visited earlier, the process takes place in a centuries-old cluster of buildings surrounded by fields of apple trees where cows graze. The giant oak barrels in dark, beamed vaults reek of age and tradition. Because of the unchanging process of manufacture and the time it takes to mature, there is a sense of timelessness about the Roger Groult distillery.

Here, in a very practical and satisfactory way, the videos and commentaries in this production centre emphasise the contrast of how things were done then and how things are done so differently now.

When grandfather Graindorge set up shop in Livarot as an *affineur* (processor and purveyor), local farmers brought their cheeses to him to ripen. Those cheeses would have been made by hand during long and laborious hours by the womenfolk. Here and now it is all about hygiene and efficiency and volume.

There are 150 suppliers of milk to the processing plant, which looks rather like a brewery with its vats and stainless steel piping. A reflection of the past is that it is still women who do the majority of the work on production and packing, but instead of milkmaid costumes they wear spotless white overalls and hats. It does not look as romantic as the tableau set in a straw-carpeted dairy at the start of the tour, but I bet the women here would rather be working in these conditions and pressing buttons and filling boxes than endlessly cranking handles and wearing a yoke like a beast of burden.

Although only coming to worldwide fame and cheese superstar status in the last century, it is thought that Livarot has been made in Normandy since at least the Middle Ages. It is part of the family of cheeses from Lower Normandy which were known to locals as *angelots*, or cherubs. To the outside world, they would become known as 'Augelots' in reference to their origins in the Pays d'Auge. In 1693, a government *intendant* (administrator) wrote about the 'extraordinary fruitfulness' of the grasslands in the area and that Livarot was known as far afield as Paris.

Although the process is in essence mechanised, the old formula is followed with animal *rennet being added to the raw milk to form curds. It is then put into moulds and next day, the unrefined cheese is salted. It will then be dried to remove excess humidity and encourage the development of yeast and mould on the surface.

Then it's time for the refining process, which begins with the traditional wrapping of individual cheeses in five strips of local sedge grass to help keep their shape. Regular washing and brushing helps the distinctive orange rind develop.

The refining or ripening of the cheese will continue after packing and dispatching, which happens after nearly a month. The strength of the odour is because Livarot is matured longer than the other cheeses of the area, and it takes a staggering five litres of milk to make just one small box.

To give an idea of the popularity of Livarot, last year eleven million litres of milk went into the production of a little over a thousand metric tons of Livarot.

We travel home laden down with samples which make the most aromatic of car air fresheners, and despite my wife's efforts with sealed plastic containers, the cabin is soon filled with the bouquet of truly ripened Livarot. There is an added bonus that the overpowering fragrance has stopped my wife complaining about the reek of my faithful old trainers.

*Animal rennet comes from the lining of the fourth stomach of a calf or certain other young beasts. The lining contains enzymes which cause milk to become cheese by separating it into curds and whey. It may seem tough on the animals involved, but cheese was still said to be the 'meat of the people' as recently as the 19th century and kept millions fed and alive.*

# Crème brûlée avec livarot, poire et noisettes

This recipe comes more or less straight from those who should know how best to make various uses of this famous cheese as it is proposed by the Graindorge Company:

## Ingredients

(for four people)
150g Livarot cheese
200g crème fraîche
Two onions
Three egg yolks
50g gingerbread
A pear
30g chopped hazelnuts
Some salt and pepper from the mill.

## Method

Remove the rind from the Livarot and chop the cheese into cubes.
Heat the crème fraîche with the Livarot in a pan.
Make a *compote of onions, pear and gingerbread separately, then mix with the cream and cheese.
Add salt and pepper to the egg yolks, beat into the mixture and pour into the ramekins.
Place in a bain-marie.
Bake at 120°C (gas mark 4) for 30 minutes.
Sprinkle with the grilled hazelnuts.

*'Compote' is French for 'mixture' and oginated in medieval Europe, where it was believed to relieve the effects of humidity on the body. It is made by simply mixing and cooking the

*ingredients over a low heat. In this case, you might want or need to add a little honey and vinegar as a liquid medium.*

# Livarot bouffées avec Calvados flambé

This is certainly not an official Graindorge-recommended dish, but one my wife devised on our return from the Livarot production centre.

When I was a child, a special treat only to be afforded at Christmastide was a tin of cheese-flavoured football-shaped puffs. Using Livarot to make puffs like these is almost like using a really expensive wine for cooking, but boy do they taste good...

## Ingredients

(for three dozen puffs)
5 tablespoons of butter
One teaspoon of salt
Quarter of a teaspoon of black pepper
Quarter of a teaspoon of freshly ground nutmeg
A cup of all-purpose flour
Five large eggs
A cup of Livarot cheese minced as fine as you can get it
Some water

## Method

Preheat your oven.
Add the butter, salt, pepper and nutmeg to a cup of water in a saucepan and bring to a boil.
Reduce heat to low and add the flour and beat for a minute or until the mixture pulls away easily from the sides of the saucepan.
Remove the pan from the heat and add the cheese.
Beat with a wooden spoon until thoroughly mixed.
Beat four of the eggs and add one at a time.
Continue beating until your mixture is shiny and firm.
Drop mixture in small spoonfuls onto a lightly greased baking

sheet.

Beat the remaining egg and use it to brush the tops of the puffs.

Bake in the oven for 15-20 minutes or until doubled in size and golden brown.

Before serving, you may choose to drizzle some Calvados over the puff and set it alight, or if like me, you find it too tricky, consume the puffs and the Calvados separately but at the same time.

# The D-Day Beaches

We rose early to share a last breakfast with our neighbours. As a treat we gave the mother duck and her brood the remnants of the Livarot cheese puffs. My wife would not allow me to carry out the Calvados flambé ceremony as it might frighten or harm the ducks, and anyway it would not be easy to set light to the puffs as they floated in the river. I offered to give them the remains of my scrambled duck eggs on toast, but my wife says that would be insensitive.

Today the plan is to visit those D-Day beaches which lay within Calvados, and after the cabin has been cleaned to my wife's satisfaction and she has re-done all the jobs entrusted to me, we take a last stroll around the lake.

I can see why so many of the caravans on this site are owned by Britons, as it is a lovely spot and ideal for exploring the rest of northern France. A mobile home is perhaps not as romantic or boast-able about, but is a lot cheaper and easier to maintain than a twee holiday cottage. Walking through the rows of caravans, you could tell the ones owned by Britons by the way tiny gardens had been established and lovingly maintained. One owner had even managed to persuade a climbing rose to thread itself around the door to his caravan. I know some people mock those who own or take their holidays in static caravans, but the mockers are the same empty-headed people who pay ludicrous amounts to spend a week in a tarted-up tent so they can tell their friends they have been 'glamping'.

Near the lake is a bar and clubroom where the British owners like to gather and moan about the French and their funny little ways. This is quite normal and natural for any expatriate people, as anyone with French friends who live in Britain will know. I think George Orwell had it right when he said in his novel *Burmese Days* that most people can be at ease in a foreign country only when disparaging the inhabitants.

This might sound a bit sweeping, but he made the observation in more colonial days. For myself, I like being in a land where attitudes, customs and sometimes behaviour can seem very foreign. Like even the most ardent Francophile, I still get peeved when confronted with examples of Gallic behaviour that do not suit me, but to plagiarise and misquote the opening lines of *The Go Between*, you have to remember and accept that France is a foreign country, and they do things differently there.

~

Mid-morning, and the Hornblowers are out in strength.

Our first encounter came when a battered pickup lurched out of a side road as we headed for the coast. I had the choice of slowing down, driving into a field or ramming the van. I chose to brake, which did not suit the driver trying to get into our boot.

A fury of beeping erupted and my pursuer got even closer to our rear bumper to harry and bully us along the narrow, single-lane stretch of road.

Eventually a suitable blind bend presented so we prepared for the inevitable. In a very French way, the driver has been enjoying sounding off at us so much that he or she had ignored several opportunities to overtake us on long, safe stretches with a clear view of what was coming up. Also, we have found that many French drivers prefer to overtake on bends and hump-back bridges or anywhere that involves the most risk and drama.

As the little Renault moved out and drew level, I saw there was actually an elderly lady at the wheel, her sharp-nosed bird-like face distended with fury. In another situation, she would have looked like someone's favourite granny; here she looked like a particularly enraged Harpy from Hell.

Suddenly, a huge blare put her honking to shame, and a giant euro-lorry filled the sky. The lady stamped on the brakes while I ignored instinct and pressed down fiercely on the accelerator. Somehow, the Renault squeezed in behind us and the lorry thundered by, all flashing lights and Doppler-effect horn.

A little further on, we saw a roadside bar. It was advertising a four-course *midi* with a bottle of wine for 12 Euros. Though a little early to eat, I pulled into the car park and unclasped my sweaty and shaking hands from the wheel. I needed a coffee, and one with a hefty shot of Calvados in it.

As we weak-knee-edly stumbled from the car, the Renault screamed by, still hooting and flashing. The driver shook a fist at me *en passant* and I realised she genuinely believed our near-death experience was my fault. I waved ironically, then pointed to where a giant combine harvester was lurching out of a field a little way ahead. This was not to warn her of the danger, but to point out another opportunity to dice with death.

~

A reminder of how relatively recently a great conflict raged here when we approach a grand *château* and see an American WWII vintage jeep standing near the gate to the driveway. It looks like it still has its original olive-green paint job, and in everyday use. This becomes clear when an elderly man in a pair of overalls of the same hue as the vehicle appears and throws a chainsaw carelessly in the back.

Intrigued, I pull over, admire the jeep and as an excuse for stopping, ask if we are on the right road to Arromanches. He says we are, but that there is a far better view of the bay if we go by the back route. With that he jumps into the jeep and roars off towards the *chateâu* in a shower of gravel, leaves and shredded bark. He lets us know we should follow with the classic wagon-train roll signal used by Robert Mitchum at the end of *The Longest Day* as he leads his troops up the hill from the beach and to victory.

# Arromanches

Our eccentric friend has left us at a vantage point overlooking Arromanches after inviting us to drop in to his home for a drop of home-brew *calva* when we are next passing.

When pressed, he admitted to being the owner of the grand *chateau*. He said he was a child when the family home was liberated from the occupying SS officers, and grew up liking British and Americans while not being too enamoured with German visitors.

He was right about the view from here, and we take in the undulating patchwork of greenery leading down to the sweeping bay, its sands dotted with what look liked abandoned fishing smacks.

In fact, they are the remains of an ingenious way of getting cargo from ship to shore after the D-Day Landings. The giant blocks of reinforced concrete had air pockets which allowed them to float. The units were made in secret locations, then sunk off the south coast of England to keep them out of sight until they were needed.

Three days after the invasion, two harbours, (codenamed Mulberry 'A' and 'B') were constructed just off Arromanches and further along the coast at Omaha Beach. The American harbour was destroyed in a storm a little more than a week later, but the other - which became known as Port Winston in honour of the Prime Minister - saw heavy use. Over ten months, it was used to land 2.5 million men, four million tons of supplies and half a million vehicles. Port Winston was created by Royal Engineers from units totalling 600,000 tons of concrete, had ten miles of floating roadways and is justly reckoned to be a truly outstanding example of military engineering.

A handful of the units did not make it across the Channel, and one lies just off-shore at my home city of Portsmouth. There is a family connection in that my father worked on building the units, and always claimed that the broken-backed casualty was one of his.

~

A decidedly frosty welcome at the tourist office at Arromanches from a sleek young woman with a long nose which she seemed to like looking down. Of course, not everyone can be polite and happy and gracious all the time and we might just have got unlucky with who was on duty when we arrived. It's possible I may have upset her by not giving the town its full name of Arromanches-les-Bains. Or perhaps my Desert Storm shorts offended her sense of fashion, or maybe her air of barely-concealed disapproval stemmed from my asking why the town had won only one flower in the Normandy Towns and Villages in Bloom competition.

Arromanches is an attractive enough place, but for the past half-hour we have been strolling along the promenade looking for somewhere to get a cup of coffee at less than high-end Paris prices. Most of the patrons are cordial, but some seem to lose interest when we say we are not eating. To be fair it is the height of the season, so they may be suffering from visitor fatigue.

We have camped at and visited Arromanches in passing a couple of times, and have to admit to mixed feelings about the place.

It may be just my mistaken perception, but the town seems keener to extract money from visitors than many other tourist destinations. Having said that, the tariff at the campsite is very reasonable. It is only a walk from the beach and run by a father-and-daughter team who could not have been more friendly and helpful.

On our last visit and when the tide was out, we would go down to the beach after the bars and restaurants had closed. With our torches marking the path, we would walk far out across the glistening stretch of sand to a world of silence. There we would climb on and inside the foreboding hulks and think about the brave men who towed the units across the Channel, and those who used them to get ashore and at the enemy.

Replete with stillness and reflection, we would return across the sand and walk along the deserted promenade, where a

German half-track carrier and a British artillery piece stand together in final harmony.

By day, we found Arromanches a much brasher place. Perhaps because of the number of eating places and bars along the promenade, the owners would compete with ever-larger signs and enticing descriptions of their wares, and not all seemed to encourage customers who are not going to spend a lot of money. In a crêperie just off the promenade, I thought the hatchet-faced woman in charge was going to call the police when I popped in and asked if we could just have a drink.

But overall, Arromanches has an important place in the recent history of Europe and America and is in the centre of the Gold Beach area, which is perhaps why so many visitors from Britain and America arrive to pay their respects and leave their money.

## Port-en-Bessin-Huppain

In the way some people add a hyphen and another name to make them sound more important and upmarket, Port-en-Bessin is now Port-en-Bessin-Huppain.

Seventy years ago it was a small and apparently insignificant fishing village, but a key objective during the D-Day landings.

The attack was made by 47 Royal Marine Commando with a force of 420 volunteers, and a small fleet of landing craft left their mother ships eight miles off the coast. Port-en-Bessin was such an important objective as it was to become the Normandy end of the PLUTO (Pipe Line Under The Ocean) operation, which would bring fuel directly from the Isle of Wight.

Almost immediately after leaving its mother ship, one of the landing craft was hit by enemy fire and sank, with twelve marines killed or drowned and eleven seriously injured. Nearing the shore, four more LCAs were impaled on submerged traps and a number of men died. Of the remaining nine landing craft, seven were too badly damaged to return to their mother ships. The order was given to surviving craft not to stop to help wounded men in the water, and a number drowned.

Port-en-Bessin and the surrounding area were taken after fierce fighting, and the cost of the operation was 48 men killed or drowned, and 70 wounded. Writing about the action, General Sir Brian Horrocks said it was doubtful whether, in their long and distinguished history, the marines had ever achieved anything finer. The historian Sir Robert Bruce Lockhart rated it as the most spectacular of all commando exploits during the invasion.

Fifty years on and twenty-odd years ago, we arrived to look round and stopped for lunch at one of the then handful of restaurants. The place we chose was tucked away behind the quayside shops and seemed to be doing its best to avoid customers, but served us a memorable meal.

It was our introduction to *raclette*, a dish from Switzerland but popular throughout France. The meal gets its name from the cheese, and is said to have come about when Swiss shepherds would put a round of raclette by the fire and scrape the melted bits on to bread. This developed into a full-blown indoors meal where the round would be set in front of an open fire, and the melted cheese served with boiled potatoes (there is a special small, sweet raclette variety), gherkins, pickled onions and any combination of cured meats. Nowadays you can buy raclette-in-a-box kits in most supermarkets, and also a specially-designed table-top electric grill. When we ate at Port-en-Bessin it was wintertime, so the cheese was melted in the traditional way before a roaring log fire. To cool us down, the meal was punctuated with regular top-ups of the traditional stone-cold stone cider cups.

What we paid then for the entire meal would probably not buy a half-bottle of wine in one of the very posh restaurants overlooking the sea nowadays. And unless we are suffering from False Memory Syndrome, the eating-houses seem to have bred and multiplied till the village looks like a scaled-down version of Honfleur.

Before leaving we walked along the quayside just to enjoy being shocked at the prices, and I lingered outside one establishment to eavesdrop on the conversation of two well-fed middle-aged men. They were studying the wine list and seemed to be taking part in some sort of bidding game, with the main rule being to find a bottle pricier than the one nominated by your opponent. When they realised I was there, the bidding became ever more intense and extravagant.

We left them working their way towards the eye-poppingly expensive section and drove back up the hill.

Times and places change and progress is usually a good thing. If you asked most of the people wining and dining outside the restaurants at the now triple-barrelled Port-en-Bessin-Huppain, I suspect they would say they like it as it is now. We preferred it as it was, but then the past invariably seems better when you look back through nostalgia-tinted glasses.

~

We head westward along a road casually littered with old guns and rusty devices which look like instruments of torture from a giant's dungeon. The great spiked harrows were probably roadblocks or tank traps, and there is even what looks like a big metal bell with slots in it at eye level. We agree it could have been a mobile pill-box, if mobile is the word.

Dotted between the rusting relics are caravans or shacks selling snacks. We pull over at the Golden Chip and try their signature dish. The lady in charge is very friendly and her *frites* are very good. Best of all is the price when compared with what a plateful would cost in more salubrious surroundings by the quayside of a nearby village. Totally irrationally, it angers me that such indulgence should take place where strangers died for freedom, and where local fishermen worked so hard and risked their lives to fill the bellies of their families.

## Omaha Beach

A selection of tanks which have not been left to the natural process of depredation guard the entrance to the stretch of coastline code-named Omaha Beach for the D-Day Invasion.

Omaha was divided into ten beaches and H-Hour was 0630. The operation involved over 30,000 men and 3000 vehicles, and the primary objective of the landing was to secure a beachhead of five miles between Port-en-Bessin and the Vire River.

The assault was led by two infantry divisions and nine companies of US Rangers.

Opposing the landing was the German 352nd Infantry Division, an uneasy mix of untested young men and battle-hardened veterans from the Eastern Front.

Very little went as planned on the day, and the defences were strong and the resistance heavy. Just trying to imagine what it would have been like to be on board one of the fleet of landing craft makes the heart race. Ten of the boats were swamped by rough seas before reaching the shore, and troops had to use their helmets to bale out and keep others afloat. Seasickness was rife and as men floundered in the water they came under increasingly heavy fire from automatic weapons and artillery. By the end of the long day, 2,499 American troops had been killed in winning the beach.

Apart from the guardian tanks and some tenacious debris, most of the evidence of that fierce conflict has gone, along with the shingle banks removed by engineers after D-Day. Many of those who gave their lives that day lie in the American Cemetery on a bluff overlooking the scene of so much terror, death and bloodshed.

As we stood and looked out over the gently rolling waves, two coaches pulled up at the monument. One carried French schoolchildren to whom the events on that day must seem as distant as some ancient battle between knights on horseback. The other coach was flying the American flag, and had brought relatives of those who fought and died here. Three very elderly men were being pushed to the monument in wheelchairs and one was making his own slow way. For them, the events of the 6th June 1944 would have been much more recent and still terrifyingly real.

## Pointe du Hoc

Further westwards and more reminders of a time when this peaceful coastal area became a place of bloody and unrelenting battle.

At a hundred feet, the Pointe du Hoc is the highest point between Omaha and Utah beaches, which straddle the border between Cavados and La Manche. On D-Day the headland was thought to be bristling with heavy guns, though most had in fact been removed after an Allied air attack in early 1944. However, the beaches at Ponte du Hoc were still under the threat of the battery at nearby Maisy.

At H-Hour on D-Day, a dozen landing craft carrying troops, amphibian vehicles, supplies and hundred-foot ladders (borrowed from the London Fire Brigade) set out for the shore. One carrying troops sank with the loss of all but one man, and another was swamped. Half the original force reached the beach, and rocket launchers were used to fire grappling hooks and ropes to the top of the cliff. It was only when the ladders were put up that they were found to be too short.

The assault was successful, but the original landing force of more than 225 was reduced to ninety. With the bitter irony of wartime operations, it was only when the men reached the top of the cliffs that they realised most of the guns they had come to destroy were no longer there.

# Grandcamp-Maisy

After all the reminders of the brutality and often futility of war, here stands a giant statue proclaiming the virtues of Peace.

Just to the east of the Calvados-La Manche border, Grandcamp-Maisy was a tiny part of the German *Atlantikwall*, put in place between 1942 and 1944 to guard against an Allied invasion. The town of Maisy was of strategic importance as it overlooks the Baie du Grand Vey and the estuary of the Vire. Three gun batteries were installed here, and defended by minefields and anti-tank lines. Some historians claim that the virtually gun-less Pointe de Hoc was used by the Germans as a ruse to distract the Allies from the batteries at Maisy.

The town is now distinguished as the site of a World Peace statue, created and donated by the Chinese Yao Yuan. The eight-ton, stainless-steel creation is an impressive structure which represents a young woman releasing the dove of peace.

The statue was unveiled in 2004, and nearby is a monument commemorating the extraordinary bravery of a US soldier. The remarkable Sergeant Frank Peregory was with the 29th Infantry Division, and two days after the D-Day Landings he single-handedly attacked a fortified machine-gun post, killing eight and capturing thirty-five German soldiers. He was killed in action six days later.

Nowadays, Grandcamp-Maisy is a peaceful place, home to two thousand inhabitants and with an active fishing port. You can eat the fruits of the local waters at any of the many restaurants in the attractive centre, visit an oyster farm, take a carriage ride or visit the Ranger Museum or the remains of a German battery. Altogether it is a busy, friendly little town and hard to associate with what happened here and along the coast only three generations ago.

# Tartlettes d'Huître,

## à la mode Normand

Perhaps understandably, there is always dispute as to the relative qualities of oysters from different parts of France. In Normandy, it can get down to what part of which *département* they are from.

In La Manche it is east coast versus west, with size, plumpness and texture contested in a generally good-natured spirit. In Calvados, the co-operatives working along the Baie des Veys say they have the perfect combination of mineral nutrients from the sea and the rich sediment from the estuary banks. Wherever they are from, this is an old Norman way of enjoying them:

## Ingredients

(to serve four)
Two dozen oysters
A litre of *mussels
100g shelled prawns
100g button mushrooms
A lemon
A bottle of dry white wine
A shallot
Some crème fraîche
100g butter
Eight short-crust pastry tartlets
Seasoning

## Method

Put the finely chopped shallot in a saucepan, with some pepper and white wine and bring to the boil.

Put in the mussels and cook over a strong heat for eight minutes.

In another saucepan, put some lemon juice and a glass of water and add the mushrooms.

Cook them for several minutes.

Meanwhile, shell the mussels and carefully strain the juice and put to one side.

Open the **oysters and put the juice into a pan.

Add the oysters and simmer for four minutes.

Strain the mushrooms and the oysters, reserving the juice.

Pour the mussel juice into a pan with the oyster juice and half the liquid from the mushrooms.

Reduce the liquid severely and add some crème fraîche and reduce until the mixture thickens.

Remove the pan from the heat and add the butter, cut into small pieces. The sauce must not boil.

Add the mussels, oysters, prawns and mushrooms to the sauce, and heat gently without boiling.

Fill the heated tartlets and serve hot with a nice bottle of white wine.

*In France, few are the supermarkets without mountains of mussels on show at a bargain price. If you have never prepared and cooked mussels, you can buy them shelled and in vacuum packs, but it is so much more fun doing it yourself. Just put them in a colander and rinse and scrub well and remove any growths or things which look like they should not be there. This will be very unlikely with farmed mussels. They will probably have been 'de-bearded' but just check. If there are any wispy little growths along the joint, pull them off.

Now this is the important bit: Mussels go off very quickly when dead, and the only obvious sign they have expired is, as with other shellfish, when they are open. However, not every open mussel is a dead mussel and it may be just having a rest. If you knock an open one against a hard surface a couple of times it may close. If it does it is still alive. If not, it is a goner and you should chuck it away. The cooking bit could hardly be simpler.

\*\*For me, opening oysters is at the same time as hard and as easy as the experts make it look. We have a special short-bladed and deliberately blunt oyster-opening knife, and I think it was a good investment. There are demonstrations and instructions aplenty online, but basically, the rules are:

1. Position the oyster in your hand with a piece of cloth round it to stop it slipping and the flat side up. Keep it level all the while so the juice will not be lost.

2. Insert your blunt but thin and pointy knife into where the shells meet and near the hinge. Then slip it in half an inch.

3. Slide the knife all around the shell join till it reaches the hinge on the other side.

4. Give the knife a bit of a twist to aid the opening process but be careful not to cause any splintering.

5. Prise the upper half of the shell fully open and use the knife to cut any muscle, being careful to remove any grit and not let it fall onto the oyster.

6. Your oyster is now open and ready for use. Do not rinse at this stage as it will spoil the flavour.

I have not bothered to tell you how to make the tartlets, as what we do is buy ready-made pastry, roll it out, put it in a tray of moulds and follow the instructions on the packet for temperatures etc.

# Isigny-sur-Mer

After a pleasant stay at a B&B on the coast, we are on the last leg of our journey around Calvados. Our first stop is at a border town said to produce the finest cream in all Normandy, if not France. I don't know about the cream or how you would judge the subtle differences, but I can vouch for the irresistible quality of the caramel sweets made here. I am not alone in my appreciation, as 300 tonnes of them change hands in the town each year.

Isigny-sur-Mer sits at the bottom of the Baie des Veys and is celebrated for its butter and cheeses as well as its cream and caramels. Along with the better-known Camembert and Pont l'Évêque, the Isigny Ste. Mère co-operative also produces Mimolette, a cheese originating from Lille. Isigny is also very big on oysters from the bay, best eaten as we did on the quay, which is lined with some fascinating old buildings. The town also has connections with the world's most famous mouse, as one Jean-Christophe d'Isigny was an ancestor of Walt D'Isney.

# Balleroy

The *château* at Balleroy is a grand affair, looking snootily down an arrow-straight driveway at the unassuming town. It was built in the 17th century from a combination of brick, schist and Caen stone and its almost matter-of-fact grandeur sums up the extremes of wealth and poverty at the time. When walking round these symbols of power and privilege, I wonder what most visitors think. Do they resent or admire the opulence, or just think how nice it would be to live in a place like that?

The grounds encircling the chateau match the splendour of the palace, and were designed by a landscape designer who was the principal gardener (if that humble word is suitable) for Louis XIV. As stately homes in England have a readily-identifiable style of gardens, so it is with France, and the grounds at Balleroy are a perfect example of the *jardin à la française*.

Inside there are paintings of Louis XIII and the family of his son, Louis XIV, and an interesting balloon museum featuring documents concerning the pioneering Montgolfier brothers.

Classified as an historic monument of France, a further claim to fame for the castle at Balleroy is that it was yet another place visited and immortalised by Marcel Proust in his never-ending novel.

## Bayeux

For me, Bayeux symbolises the past in the way that Caen, in spite of its ancient castle and long history, makes me think of now and the future.

Caen is all bustle and modernistic tall buildings and grid-like street layouts, while Bayeux reeks of history. It also has a pretty well-known embroidery which brings the distant past to life. Whatever the reason, to me Bayeux has a similar feel to an ancient British university town, where old lives with new but the past is always present.

I am also taken with Bayeux because it is where I ate the best kebab in the world, ever. There are more kebab shops even than McDonald outlets in France, but none that I have visited offers anything like Bayeux's *Kebab Normand*.

Operating from a small kiosk near the town centre, the patron is Norman rather than Turkish, and his kebabs reflect his roots. The tender slivers of locally-produced lamb are drenched in a palate-seducing sauce made from double cream and melted Camembert cheese with mushrooms fresh from the field. Forget curry and chips or bacon baguettes, that's what I call fusion cooking.

Apart from its kebabs and the Tapestry, Bayeux has lots more to offer. The feeling of a long and established history probably comes from it dating back to at least the 4th century. In 880, the town was taken by Rollo the Viking, and subsequently became a Norman stronghold. Luckily for the inhabitants and future visitors, Bayeux was one of the few larger Norman towns emerging relatively unscathed by the D-Day invasion. Whether this is because it was the first main town to be liberated I do not know.

Happily, as a result the centre is crammed with striking half-timbered buildings dating back to the 13th century. There's also the Gothic cathedral, and I particularly like the Botanical gardens and especially the small but perfectly formed waterway that winds its way through the town centre, pretending to work ancient mill wheels on route. In common with many towns with lots of history and activities and visitors, Bayeux seems much bigger than its population of 15000 would suggest.

~

Of course, the reason that so many people come to Bayeux is the eponymous Tapestry.

It is, as every schoolboy and girl knows - or should know - an alleged record of the events leading up to and after the Battle of Hastings and the start of the Norman Occupation of Saxon Briton. I say alleged because, quite naturally, history is always written - or in this case embroidered - by the winners.

Unlike the Shroud of Turin or the moon landings, nobody has ever suggested that the tapestry is a fake, though its origins are disputed. Some experts stick to the belief that it was the work of William the Conqueror's wife, Queen Matilda. Not that she actually sat and made it herself, of course, but that she had the Big Idea. Others claim it was commissioned by Odo, Bishop of Bayeux and half-brother to William. Whatever the true origins and verity of the scenes displayed, it is an awe-inspiring creation, and a detailed record of how people lived and, mostly, how they fought at that time.

The tapestry is not that far off a hundred yards long, and 19.5 inches in depth. It was made of a seamless strip of linen, embroidered with eight colours of woollen thread. The strip shows 72 individual scenes and 1512 figures, with 'captions' in Latin. The panels tell the story - from a Norman perspective - of King Harold's refusal to honour his oath of recognition that his cousin William should succeed Edward the Confessor, and how William set out in 1066 to claim his prize.

This was our third visit to gawp at the tapestry, but our first in the heat of the tourist season.

The Tapestry attracts 400,000 visitors a year, and we had chosen to arrive after lunch in mid-August. By my reckoning that meant several hundred people were being processed every hour along the dimly-lit viewing corridor. It was very efficiently and effectively done, allowing that most French people think queues are for wimps. Having no choice but to stand in line for more than a hundred metres, some naturally had a problem understanding that the point of this queue was not to get to the other end as soon as possible.

A complication was that we had chosen to wear the sophisticated headsets which tell you about the contents of each panel as you reach it. With continuous pressure from behind, the problem was in having a chance to look at a panel and listen to what it represented before we were shepherded forward by the people behind. In a way it was a bit like driving on a French country lane with Hornblowers lining up behind you. Wanting my money's worth, I literally dug my heel in about half way along the stretch, which caused a significant gap to appear. This was filled by people behind losing patience and doing a typical French overtaking manouvre which ended with cutting sharply in front of us to show their displeasure at being held up.

In the end, trying to follow the description of a scene three panels back or two in front was sometimes like watching a movie where the sound is out of synch. But it was still an awe-inspiring experience. Sometimes familiarity can take the shine off a place or object; in this case it was like watching a really good movie for the third time and seeing lots of things you had missed last time round. Still wondering at how close the distant past can be made to seem, we finally let ourselves be carried along by the flow of humanity through the souvenir shop and out into the bright sunshine.

This will be our last night in Calvados, so we need to return to the excellent camp site and dress up for a celebration meal. There are more than a hundred restaurants in Bayeux, some of which come highly recommended on those often irritating amateur reviewers' sites. Our choice of establishment is not mentioned on any, but this evening we will be dining *en plein air* in the Botanical gardens, and on a traditional *Kebab Normand*.

# Calvados Soufflé

There's a restaurant in Orbec famed for its soufflé with Calvados. The recipe was devised by chef Didier Tricot at the Caneton restaurant.

'Soufflé' comes via Latin to the French to puff or blow up (as in inflate), and is used as slang for the breathalyser. A soufflé can be either sweet or savoury and the invention (or at least the popularising) of this famously tricky dish is generally attributed to the great chef Carème. Others say the dish first arrived on Parisian plates as early as the end of the 17th century.

One thing we all know about a soufflé is that timing is all and you don't get a second shot if it all goes pear-shaped. But to put one old excuse to bed, sound cannot make a soufflé collapse.

Generations of chefs have blamed kitchen assistants for slamming a door or shouting at the crucial moment, but I am assured by the scientific community that it is a temperature and not a noise problem which makes a gloriously fluffy soufflé become a pancake.

## Ingredients

For the pastry cream:
Half a litre of unpasteurised milk (if you can get it)
Four eggs
55g plain flour
200g caster sugar
Also:
Eight egg whites
Six yolks
Eight *Boudoir biscuit halves
Some Calvados
Eight soufflé moulds

## Method

Soak the biscuits in Calvados.
Make the *pastry cream and leave to cool.
Prepare the soufflé moulds by buttering and then dusting them with sugar.
Now add the six egg yolks to the pastry cream when it is cold.
Preheat the oven to $200^0$C.
Before baking, whip the egg whites into peaks with a pinch of salt, then slowly add to the pastry cream.
Half-fill the moulds, add the biscuits and then fill the moulds to the top.
Cook for 15 to 20 minutes depending on your oven.

*Pastry cream or 'crème pât' is a staple in French pâtisserie work and is what we would call thick custard. It is made by whisking together the eggs and sugar until it reaches a pale gold colour, then whisking in the flour before setting aside. Bring the milk to simmering point in a heavy-bottomed saucepan, then remove from the heat and leave for thirty seconds. Slowly pour half the hot milk into the egg mixture while whisking all the time, then slowly add the remaining milk. It is important to pour the hot milk slowly on to the cold eggs or they will scramble. Bring the mixture to the boil and simmer while whisking for a minute or until the mixture thickens. Then pour the mixture into a bowl. It is a good tip to dust the surface of your custard with a little icing sugar to prevent a skin forming. Finally, put the bowl containing the crème pât into a bigger bowl of iced water to aid the cooling process.
NB. I note that M. Tricot does not include icing sugar or vanilla in his recipe ingredients for the crème pât, so neither have I.

*Boudoir biscuits may also be known as Savoiardi, Naples biscuits or the more down-to-earth 'ladyfingers' in the UK. They originate from the court of the Duchy of Savoy in the late 15th century created to mark a visit by the King of France. In his recipe, M. Tricot suggests you might wish to substitute the *biscuits for eight génoise cakes, which as the name suggests, are Italian sponge cakes which originated in Genoa.*

# MANCHE

As well as the name of a department in Lower Normandy, Manche ('the sleeve') is what the French call the stretch of water which for some reason they refuse to refer to as the English Channel.

Attitudes have changed greatly over the years, but too many Britons still seem to think that Manche is too close to Britain to be properly French. Contrary to their bizarre belief, Real France does not commence somewhere around the Loire Valley and become more French the further south you go. Believe me, France really does start at Cherbourg.

As the Cotentin peninsula is surrounded on three sides by water, it is no surprise that the department is known for the use it makes of the fruits of the sea. Inland, the rich earth provides beef and milk and apples and cider and Calvados and cattle corn aplenty. The peninsula, as we shall discover, has a particularly rich and turbulent history and was home to many a warlord and his fiefdom.

Other parts of France may offer more popular weather or more spectacular topographical features, but Manche is replete with history, great food, drink and gorgeous places to visit. In short, it is a small but perfectly formed microcosm of all the best bits of France. We love every inch of the Cotentin, but have every reason to be biased.

*Author's note: As our love affair with Normandy and France began in this department, my first seven books naturally focused on our life and times in the Cotentin peninsula. Happily, most of our favourite places have changed little across the years, and, where I think apt I have dropped in brief extracts from the Mill of the Flea series. If nothing else, they give an indication of how I saw those people and places then. They are in a different type face and separated from the body copy with lines just to ensure you do not think I am writing about modern times.*

# Cherbourg

We are on very familiar territory, but there are other reasons we feel at home in this *city by the sea.

Cherbourg and our home town of Portsmouth face each other across seventy miles of seaway and are similar in a number of ways. They are both major naval and ferry ports which were knocked about a bit in the War, and both suffer from some monstrously ugly quick-fix buildings thrown up after the end of hostilities.

Both share the same weather and have lots of pubs and restaurants. However, the only young females you are likely to find lying in a pool of their own vomit after a night out are likely to be in Portsmouth shop doorways. Unless, that is, they have come over the Channel via the Portsmouth ferry port.

For some reason, apart from a slightly louche feel and the booze cruisers that used to plague the waterfront areas of the town, Cherbourg seems not to be universally admired by the rest of France. In fact, it has been known for some French people to refer to Cherbourg as the bum-hole of France. I am told this is not so much as an insult as it would be in English. It is said because, being at the top of the Cotentin peninsula, Cherbourg is the last stop in France before the barbarian territories of southern England.

Clearly, anyone who is not a fan of this sometimes edgy city by the sea has not taken the time and trouble to get to know the place properly, and there is a lot more to Cherbourg than immediately meets the eye.

Nowadays and in line with the current fad for double-barreled names, the town is officially referred to as Cherbourg-Octeville. Because of the joining-up of the two communities, it has now become the most populous town in the department, and sometimes feels it when you are down in the docks area and trying to cross a busy road.

For obvious reasons, Cherbourg has always been a key strategic location and was known as one of the 'keys to the kingdom'.

Because of this, massive sea defences were added until, by the middle of the 19th century, Cherbourg boasted the biggest man-made harbour in the world.

As well as a string of foreign invaders, the port has also been a stop-off point for all sorts of more friendly visitors. In 1912, the SS Titanic called here before heading off on its fateful journey.

By the first half of the 20th century, state-of-the-art transatlantic liners would heave-to at the magnificent art-deco terminal which now hosts the impressive *Cité de la Mer*. Hollywood stars would regularly be aboard, and older Cherbourgois are proud that the likes of Elizabeth Taylor and Rita Hayworth set foot here.

The town was a primary objective for the D-Day invasion, but it is a little known fact that, at one time, Americans were fighting between themselves just off the peninsula.

The Battle of Cherbourg was a single-ship action between two sloops-of-war in 1864, from which the Union vessel emerged triumphant. Another suitably quirky claim to fame for the town is that Napoleon's ashes passed through Cherbourg en route to Paris in 1840 after his death on St Helena. This explains the statue on the promenade which has the Little Emperor sitting on his favourite horse and pointing directly across the Channel at Britain.

Altogether, with its colourful history, modern buzz and the sometimes edgy feel that ports and dockside cities can have, Cherbourg is right up our street.

~

Our love affair with Cherbourg and then Normandy in general began in 1986, when I escorted a thousand pub landlords and their spouses on a booze cruise to remember. Or, in some cases, not to remember.

I was editor of *Food & Drink Magazine* and my business partner and I had come up with a proposal for the mighty Whitbread brewery company. We thought it would make a great feature for the magazine and a nice profit for us if we arranged it. Our proposal was not of course in the same league as the D-day landings, but in retrospect perhaps nearly as risky as to chances of success.

The plan was to hire a P&O ferry for 24 hours and turn the car deck overnight into a temporary exhibition hall. After filling the space with stalls showing off the full range of Whitbread-supplied beers, wines and spirits, we would set out for Cherbourg on a day trip. Then there would be some free time ashore in Cherbourg, and then the tenant licensees would be returned to Portsmouth having had a great day out and ordering lots of drinks from the exhibitors on board.

The weather on the day was obviously going to be a significant factor, so to publicise the event I dressed up as a Norse warrior and (allegedly) broke a barrel of lager over the bows of the SS Viking Victory. The press release claimed this was how Vikings propitiated their gods in the hope of a successful raping, pillaging but storm-free voyage. I had made it all up, but together with the photograph of the scantily-clad Vikingette in my arms, the story did the trick and got massive media coverage.

On the big day, the band played and streamers and the odd beer bottle were thrown on to the quayside, and the SS Viking Victory steamed from Portsmouth into the record books as the world's first-ever **cross-Channel trade fair. On the car deck, the marketing men were kept busy giving out samples of leading bottled and draught beers and spirits at a rate which would have gladdened the heart of any pub landlord. During the outward crossing our guests got through thousands of glasses of booze, and the P&O bursar said he was unhappy at our giving away free drinks as that would obviously impact on sales at the bar.

In response, I simply asked him when they had last had a thousand professional drinkers on board, and by the time the boat arrived back in Portsmouth, the bars had taken more money in one crossing than in the history of the Peninsular and Orient shipping company.

We arrived safely in Cherbourg, and while the licensees went in search of quayside bars in which to slake their thirsts, my wife and I stood in front of an estate agent's window and goggled at the prices of property. The average going rate seemed about a fifth the cost in France for a like-for-like home on our side of the Channel. We had always wanted a house in the country but had never been able to afford one. Now it seemed we could, though it would mean that our second home would have to be in another country.

Not long after that life-changing day, Cherbourg became our second-home home town. This is a sample of my early impressions from a series of memoirs about our time in Normandy.

Cherbourg has changed since then, but thankfully not that much:

---

I do enjoy walking the streets as Cherbourg wakes.

As we make our way across the Turning Bridge, gulls wheel overhead and seem to be laughing harshly at some private joke as they swoop down to seek pickings in the overflowing bins outside restaurants and bars. The occasional car races by in search of an unwary cyclist or pedestrian, and small groups of dishevelled Britons look for an English-style pub so they can refuel before catching the early morning ferry back to their real worlds.

Although it has not been raining, the pavements gleam from the attentions of a council worker astride his ingenious water-spraying machine, and trolleys of fresh fruit, vegetables and fish are being wheeled into shops along the quayside. I breathe in the morning air, and savour the heady fusion of aromas coming from the sea, freshly-brewed coffee, baking bread, stale tobacco and urine which means we could be nowhere else in the world but a French port.

*Home & Dry in France*

---

*You may have noticed that I tend to duck and dive about with my references to the same place as a town or city. I do so when I want to distinguish between a small town like St. Mere-Eglise or a very big one like Caen. The thing is that the French refer to all their centres of population which are not hamlets or villages as towns regardless of size, and that includes Paris. Having said that, their marketing slogan for Cherbourg refers to 'the city by the sea.'*

\*\*Despite our fears we left only one passport-less pub landlord stranded on the quayside at Cherbourg. On the plus side there was little vandalism, no arrests and hardly any fights in the town. Best of all, the sea was flat calm and everyone said they had a lovely time. But the cross-channel trade show was not an unqualified success with regard to all its objectives.

The dual aims of the exercise (apart from us making lots of money from it) had been to win goodwill and increased future drinks orders as a result of the sampling of company products. But my partner and I (and our sponsors) had forgotten one simple fact: Alcoholic drinks bought from French supermarkets are a lot cheaper than they are in Britain, even if you are a publican buying direct from a brewery. As a result, many of the licensees armed themselves with shopping bags on wheels, suitcases, supermarket trolleys and in one case a commodious wheelbarrow and came straggling back on board towing huge quantities of duty-free booze. As it was and is illegal to sell French-bought drinks over the bar counter, the licensees assured the brewery management that it was all for personal consumption. Despite this, drinks orders from the landlords to the brewery in the month following the voyage were surprisingly low.

We have taken the coastal road eastward along the top end of the peninsula, in some stretches and apart from the weather, the winding road beside soaring granite overhangs and cliffs falling away to the attractively marbled green and blue waters could be in Spain rather than Northern France.

On our way to a port bursting with history, we pass through a number of small villages, all minding their own businesses and not too fussed about tourists or summer visitors. That's another thing we like about Lower Normandy

## Phare de Gatteville

Millions of sailors and ferry passengers will know or have seen the probing beam of the *phare* at Gatteville. At 75 metres or a shade under 250 feet, it is the third tallest 'traditional' lighthouse in the world, and the light was first lit in 1775.

With many submerged rocks and strong and awkward currents, this part of the northern coast had long been a graveyard for shipping. The most famous casualty was the *Blanche-Nef* or White Ship in 1120. On the 25th of November, the man at the tiller was the son of the captain of the vessel which took William the Conqueror towards Hastings and his and England's destiny. The VIP passenger was William Ætheling, the only legitimate heir of Henry I of England. His death when the White Ship was lost off Barfleur led to the succession crisis and a period of civil war in England known as The Anarchy.

Whether by design or coincidence, the lighthouse at Gatteville has a step for every day of the year, and it has been a tradition for us to climb them at least once a year. As time has passed, it seems to me that more steps are being sneakily added, and this was the first visit where I had to give in and take a breather before reaching the top.

On the way back down, we passed other sufferers, mostly huddled in passing niches and having a cigarette to get their breaths back. Smoking gave me up five years ago, which still probably accounts for my failure to reach the top of the lighthouse. I did ask a large woman sucking on a Gitane if I could have a drag, but my wife propelled me on down the remaining steps with a shove that could have been more fatal than me taking up the habit again.

## Barfleur

If you were a researcher looking for the perfect set for a film about the goings-on at a quaint but proper working French fishing port, you would need to look no further than Barfleur. It is that unusual hybrid of a tourist venue which still makes a living out of the ancient occupation which makes it so attractive to visitors.

In fact, Barfleur goes back a long way, and was once much more than a fishing village. It was one of the chief ports for travel to and from England long before Cherbourg got into the act. There is a plaque on the slipway registering the departure of vessels bound for the Battle of Hastings, and Richard the Lionheart regularly passed through on his way to and from slaughtering Muslims in the Crusades.

What is especially appealing about Barfleur is that the town has not encroached on the port, nor has the quay become an isolated and over-commercialised mini-Honfleur awash with posh eateries. The rusty anchor chains, coils of frayed rope and lobster pots have not been placed there for effect, and the old granite houses with white shutters huddled around the quayside are mostly lived in by real people and not holiday-home owners. Some of the cottages bear plaques noting the famous people who have dwelled in them, and one of them was the future Archbishop of Canterbury and ill-fated Thomas Beckett. Away from the quayside, a small skein of narrow alleyways leading to the quay and the interestingly cupola-domed and one-time fortified church.

But the port is not just about the past, and lines of refrigerated lorries daily line the water's edge to take the famous Barfleur mussels to all parts of France. When the tide is right, you will also see locals with buckets and waders harvesting the wild oysters and mussels.

We once had a feast of wild oysters at what was then reckoned to be Barfleur's top restaurant, and they were as big as fried eggs. As the chef gathered them in person, they were also much more expensive than the cultivated variety, but luckily we were guests of a French journalist writing about the mad Englishman who preferred to live in Manche in a ruined watermill than a comfortable modern house.

## La Pernelle

Just a few miles due south of Barfleur is La Pernelle, an inland village distinguished by having one of the smallest town halls in all France. It also has an impressive grotto dedicated to Our Lady of Lourdes, and one of the most striking panoramic views in the peninsula. From in front of the old church, you can see right across the fields and bay to an interesting and eye-pleasing island.

The Ile de Tatihou occupies little more than seventy acres, and is virtually uninhabited. It is accessible by walking between oyster beds at low tide, or there is a sort of giant-wheeled amphibious bus which ferries visitors the short distance from the shore. There is a botanical garden to visit, and an ornithological reserve on the island which is a stopping-off point for many migrating species. There's also a folk festival each year which is timed to agree with the tides, but there's a limit of 500 visitors a day all year round.

Place names throughout the peninsula betray its Norse heritage, and the suffix –hou means 'small island'. For once, the twinning authorities got it absolutely right with Tatihou, which is linked with Brownsea Island off Dorset.

## Saint-Vaast-la-Hougue

If there is a yachtie heaven in this part of the peninsula, it has to be Saint-Vaast-la-Hougue. Expensive houses, expensive boats and even a very expensive grocery store. You are nobody in yachting circles if you have not done St Vaast and can drop the name of the town and its hazards casually in to the conversation at your sailing club.

With no justification I feel much more drawn to honest, working-class Barfleur, and would rather be given a disparaging once-over by a chunky fisherman than a snotty yachtie who thinks he is better than me because he can look as if he knows what to do with a bit of nylon rope.

The fisherman who lives locally and knows and works the

dangerous seas for a living is entitled - to my mind - to ignore or look down his nose at any day tripper. Unless he has sailed round the world on his own, fought off whales and lived on ship's biscuit for a year, I don't see why a person should think himself better than me because he has a pair of yellow wellies. But perhaps it is just my reverse snobbery that drives my innate distaste for leisure sailors.

Talking of snobbery, Saint-Vaast is the home to a grocery shop which makes Harrods Food Hall look like a down-market branch of Kwik Save.

Founded by Clovis Gosselin in 1899, Maison Gosselin is world-famous, probably in some degree due to leisure sailors spreading the word about how much it is possible to pay for stuff there. I never pass this way without going in and trying to look as if I mean to buy something as I wander and wonder through row after row of comestibles and luxury goods. I think the best description I have read of the premises was in a travel guide which said that the art of presenting the most common objects as the rarest had been transmitted from generation to generation. Personally, I am full of admiration for any family business which makes a great success, and especially one which manages to persuade people to pay through the nose for sometimes everyday objects. Especially as a lot of the customers will be snotty yachties.

**Public Apology**: After sneering at the soft-handed yachtspersons who flock there - and by implication dissing the place itself - I owe Saint-Vaast-la-Hougue a contrite apology. Talking to a local historian recently, I learned that in medieval times the twee sailing venue was the site of perhaps the toughest of all seagoing activities. He assured me that the port once had a thriving whaling community. Apparently, the local waters were thick with the gray whale, now extinct in the Atlantic. The good news is that some of the species have found their way through the ice-free Northwest Passage, so may appear again.

# Brix

I love it when improbable legend proves to be historical fact.

Just up the road from where we lived for many years, Brix is a pleasant little village tucked away in the heart of the peninsula. It has a couple of bars and shops, a very good bakery and a solid-looking church. Brix sits at a high point, and has always reminded me of what I think a rugged Scottish hilltop village should look like, especially when it rains.

In the early days of our time living in Manche, we were told by an elderly member of the Néhou Jolly Boys Club (*see later*) that the village was once the fief of an ancestor of the great Scottish hero, Robert the Bruce. As conclusive evidence, the old countryman pointed out that 'Brix' was pronounced 'Broo' in the Cotentin version of Norman patois. That alone proved Robert the Bruce was actually Robert of Brix.

I paid the usual fee of a shot of home-brew *calva* for this piece of local lore, but never really took it on board. When you think I was also asked to believe that one of the oldest members of our unofficial social club was immortal and a drinking mate of William the Conqueror, you can perhaps see why I took the tale with a pinch of salt.

Then, some years later, old Pierrot was proved right.

There were general celebrations in historical circles when the heart of Robert the Bruce was rediscovered during an archeological dig in Scotland in 1996, and the media was full of stories about the man and his ancestry. It was revealed that the first Robert arrived in Normandy from Great Britain sometime in the mid -11th century and took Brix as his fiefdom. He joined William for the Battle of Hastings, and was rewarded with vast estates to the north of the conquered realm.

By the time his tall tale was vindicated, I could not apologise to old Pierrot as he, unlike his fellow member, had proved not to be immortal. I did, however, apologise to his shade and toasted his memory at an extra-curricular meeting of the Jolly Boys Club

~

The RN 13 (*Route Nationale*) trunk road runs due south from Cherbourg, linking Cotentin to the rest of France. A few miles from the town and on the northbound carriageway is a small blue, home-made sign advertising the services of a Château B&B. Seeing the simple sign kick-starts a treasure-chest of memories for me.

The website for the Chateau Le Mont Epinguet describes the premises as 'informal' and the owner is one of the most informal people I have known.

I first met Mark Berridge when he was a property agent, finding homes for British would-be expatriates or *résidence secondaire* owners. It was he who found us two much-loved homes in Cotentin, one of which we sold while the paint was literally still drying on the walls. The other proved to be our property love of a lifetime, but more of that anon.

At first sight, Mark did not look like your typical estate agent. He wore an endless Dr Who scarf, a philosopher's fedora hat, odd socks and the thoughtful look of a man who thinks he may have left a cake in the oven on the planet Zog.

Apart from his outward appearance, I thought Mark was not suited for his job; this was because he was totally honest, which is not a virtue normally associated with estate agents. Not only would he not skate over or neglect to mention problems with a house he was selling, but he would actually point out any defects that the viewer might not have spotted. At heart, he was a matchmaker, intent on introducing the right people to the right property... for them.

When customers bought a place he believed suited them, he would celebrate. When they insisted on buying somewhere that he thought did not match their character, means or needs, he would attend the exchange as if it were a wake and not a wedding. He once politely opined that our modest homes in Cotentin were too small for my personality, and took us to view a huge stately home in a very bad way. There was nothing in it for Mark except the satisfaction of making a good match, and it could have been ours for a song. As he cheerfully pointed out, it would be the best part of a lifetime's work to put it right, but to see it restored to life and fulfillment would be a reward beyond compare. I chickened out of taking on the challenge, but over time came to realise he had been completely right.

In his time, Mark has found homes on the peninsula for thousands of Brits, and dissuaded almost as many from choosing the wrong place for them. He has painted a *château* pink in a good cause, and converted a former SS torture chamber into a tasteful *gîte*. Along the way, he and his wife Fiona created an internationally acclaimed hospitality business.

The Château le Mont Epinguet once belonged to a French admiral, and came to Mark in a far-from-perfect state. I did not see him or his wife out of overalls for the best part of a decade, and the weight of taking on collapsing roofs and floors and dry and wet rot would have crushed a lesser couple. Now, Mont Epinguet is celebrated by critics and visitors alike as a conference or holiday centre for hire, but for me it will always be a gloriously eccentric B&B in the grandest of surroundings.

We have dropped in not only to see our old friends, but to pick up the Tardis.

Coming off the production line at the same time as actor Bruce Willis had an unlikely hit with *Under the Boardwalk* and before even the first *Die Hard* was made, The Conway Tardis was a tribute to British design and ingenuity several decades ago. Technically it is known as a trailer-tent, but I prefer to think of it as an exploding caravan with a hard top and a soft centre. To the untrained eye it looks like any other modest trailer, sitting innocently behind the car awaiting a stack of boxes, a heap of rubble or a *dead pig. But, within minutes of arriving on site, retractable legs have been lowered, catches un-catched, crank-handles cranked and a fair sized, fabric-walled caravan has taken shape by sprouting out of the trailer like a very magic mushroom on an amphetamine-based compost. Living up to its name, the Tardis offers a seating area with table, a wardrobe and lots of storage space, two bedrooms and a kitchen with all cons that were mod in 1987.

We acquired Dodo (named after a Dr Who assistant in the Sixties and not because the brand was technically extinct) some years ago when, as you do, I met an adventurous vicar at a book-signing session in Brittany. In conversation he mentioned that he had bought a new caravan and was looking for a good home and caring hands for his old trailer-tent.

A deal was struck on the spot, with the good reverend walking away with a complete set of my books, and us taking possession of the Tardis.

We obviously got much the better of the deal and had years of enjoyment upsetting snooty caravan owners by parking next to them. But the old girl is now showing her years and getting a bit shaky. There are leaks in the roof, a couple of side panels have gone missing and the wheels wobble a bit at anything over five miles an hour. We could think of no better retirement home than one of the outbuildings at the Château B&B, and Mark has been taking good care of Dodo. But as we are taking a sentimental journey for the last leg of our tour of Lower Normandy, we thought it fitting to give Dodo one more taste of freedom and the open road.

Hitched up and ready to go, we said goodbye to our old friend and headed for the Little Jewel, which was a perfect example of Mark Berridge's uncanny talent for matching people with property that will steal their hearts.

*I have in fact seen dead pigs transported by trailer in the Cotentin. In fact I have seen live cows being carried to market this way, and it is a unique experience to make eye-contact with one as the owner overtakes you on a blind bend in the pre-dawn hours. To add to my collection of Unusual and Exceptional Toilets, I plan one day to publish a short monograph on Things I have Seen in Trailers.

## Valognes

Before the onslaught of the D-Day Landings, Valognes was known as the Versailles of the North. I don't know how well it deserved that comparison or if it was the invention of a switched-on 19th century marketing man, but there are certainly no palaces here now.

Over the years the town has seen its fair share of action, and it was at Valognes that William the Conqueror learned that the local barons were conspiring to do him in. Edward II of England stayed the night here, then casually pillaged the town. Later on, Henry III held Valognes for thirty years, and treated it a bit better. Before the Revolution, more than a hundred aristocratic and stupendously wealthy families had splendid homes in and around the town, which is obviously where the marketing man got his Versailles idea from.

Valognes is one of the several thousands of small French towns which are dubbed as 'typical' by people who, like me, write travel literature. This of course is not true or fair, as every small French town is unique.

Nowadays, the town sits comfortably around a square where the weekly market is held. There is the odd old building, and a college and a train station, and for tourists there are two museums dedicated to the history of cider and apple brandy. Just out of town there's a pretty former mill where descriptions of dozens of crêpes and galettes with different fillings adorn the menu. At a former forge on the outskirts, we have shared a gigantically juicy *côte de bouef* cooked to perfection over an open fire, and the memory returns every time we drive by.

More nostalgically and even though nobody has put a blue plaque on the notary's wall, Valognes is where we signed the forms which allowed us to pick up the keys to our first home in France.

# The Little Jewel

Not long after the publican's booze-cruise day to Cherbourg, I pulled off a deal in which a parcel of pubs changed hands and we suddenly had enough money to buy a cheap new car, or even a very modest holiday home in France. The holiday home won hands down, which is how we came to be the owners of a tiny 19th-century cottage in a hamlet outside Valognes. It was love at first site, as Mark Berridge had come up trumps with a bijou dwelling stuffed with character and some interesting and even intriguing features.

Peeling from the walls were sodden strips of wallpaper representing English hunting scenes, and the only personal hygiene facility was a sort of plastic telephone box plumbed in as a shower to the centre of the tiny kitchen. Also in the kitchen was a door leading to the strangest and most potentially lethal toilet I have ever seen - and I have seen plenty. A cross between a caravan loo and the sort of pump-action device you find at sea, it had an inlet pipe connected to a water source on one side, and on the other, a narrow tube which disappeared into the two-foot thick granite outer wall. Once used, the idea was to eject the contents of the bowl through the pipe and off the premises by energetically pumping on the handle. As we were to discover, the pipe was blocked solid and there were near-catastrophic consequences when we tried to expel decades of petrified pooh, but that's another *story.

What really sold us on the Little Jewel was not the eccentricity of the facilities, but the booty from looting immediately after the French Revolution.

The sitting room was paved with massive, time-worn slabs which looked more suited to a grand *château* than a humble cottage. This was because they had been ripped out of the domicile of a local *aristo* after he had got the chop in Paris. Also from the same source was the massive stone fireplace surround, with the coat of arms of the original owner above the mantle. It looked totally out of place, but we loved it.

We made an offer on the spot, and bought *Petit Bijou* after a series of complications had been resolved. In spite of our protests, we then sold it while the paint on the walls was still drying, but that is also another story. We were always sad to have owned it only for such a short time, but as our friend and property agent Mark Berridge said, had we not moved on from The Little Jewel we would never have found and had an everlasting love affair with the Mill of the Flea.

*If you are interested in how we came to find, buy and sell the Little Jewel and end up with a ruined water mill on ten acres of fields, streams woods and mud, the full story is in Home & Dry in France, the first book in the Mill of the Flea series.*

# Coquilles Saint Jacques
## avec Cidre

The scallop shell is the symbol of St James (St.Jacques to the French), and they were mounted on posts to mark the ancient *Santiago de Compostela* pilgrim routes through France to Spain. One of the major routes for pilgrims setting out from England was across the Channel to Barfleur and down through the Cherbourg peninsula. The trail went past our farmhouse at La Puce, of which more later. This delightfully Norman-ised version uses cider rather than the white wine favoured in other parts of France:

## Ingredients

12 scallops
Two shallots
50g of unsalted butter
250ml of dry cider
Salt and pepper
A heaped teaspoon *fond de poisson*
150g of crème fraîche

*This is a rich fish stock, also known as fumet de poisson. Fish stock can be had at many suitable outlets.*

## Method

Wash the scallops and ensure that any black 'strings' are removed.

Finely chop the shallots.

Melt the butter in a heavy frying pan.

Toss in the shallots and sweat for a couple of minutes whilst stirring with a wooden spatula, then mix in the cider.

Put the scallops, salt and pepper in and cook for no more than five or six minutes for large scallops, less for small.

Drain the liquid into a small pan and keep the scallop and shallot mixture warm.

Reduce the liquid by half, then mix the *fond* with the *créme fraîche* and add to the reduced liquid.

Stir until incorporated and bring gently to simmer.

Add the scallops and shallots and serve with a slice of lemon and crusty baguette.

# Sainte-Mère-Église

The one thing people seem to know about this town is that a parachutist got caught on the church steeple during the D-Day Invasion. The other is the way John Wayne drawled 'We're gonna take Saintmaryglise' in the film *The Longest Day.*

Sitting alongside the RN13 and close to the Landing beaches, Sainte-Mère-Église was an important inland beachhead for the Allies to repulse any counter-attacks. Consequently, a mixed force of men from the US 82nd Airborne and the US Airborne Divisions made a drop on the town in the early hours of D-Day.

Operation Boston did not start well, as burning buildings illuminated the sky and made easy targets of the parachutists. Some fell into fires, others were caught up on telegraph poles and trees and shot before they could cut themselves free.

The incident that caught the public imagination involved Private John Steele of the 505th Parachute Infantry Regiment. His parachute becoming entangled with the spire of the church in the square, he was left helplessly dangling. For two hours he pretended to be dead, then was taken prisoner. He later escaped and joined comrades in capturing thirty members of the garrison force and killing eleven. Reinforcements arrived later in the morning, and held out under heavy fire for more than a day until tanks from Utah Beach arrived to relieve them.

A lesser-known friend of John Steele was demolition specialist and combat engineer Henry Langrehr, whose exploits were also recorded in *The Longest Day.*

First out of the plane, Langrehr carried a Thompson submachine gun, a 45 calibre and a 30 pound explosive charge strapped to his leg. The 150lb of equipment doubled his weight and he came down heavily, crashing through a greenhouse roof. One of the few men to survive the deadly drop, he won two Bronze Stars and Two Purple Hearts for his valour, and in 2007 was awarded France's highest honour, The Légion d'Honneur.

The first time we visited Sainte-Mère-Église was the day after the fiftieth anniversary of D-Day. It was lunchtime and the streets were near-deserted. It was a pleasant, sunny day and hard to associate this quiet little town with the horrors of war. As we crossed the square to look up at the parachute and the effigy of Pte Steele hanging beneath it, we heard a jaunty military air coming from an open window. It was the theme tune of *The Longest Day*, and the hairs on the back of my neck stood up as I tried to think what it must have been like to have come from a placid life and town in America and be dropped into an inferno of flames and fury.

~

From June 1940 to June 1944, no Allied soldier set foot on French soil.

On the 6th June 1944, the seaborne invasion was preceded by parachute drops and an intense bombardment. In all, 200,000 American, British, Canadian and Commonwealth troops came ashore.

Utah Beach was the codename for one of the five landing sectors, on the shoulder of the peninsula and stretching westward from the mouths of the Douve and Vire rivers.

D-Day began at Utah Beach at 06.30hrs, when the first of four waves of infantry and tanks secured the immediate area with surprisingly light casualty figures. Of the 21,000 troops landed on Utah, there were 197 deaths and injuries, compared with the 2,500 casualties taken by the 14000 men arriving by parachute and glider.

The reason for the ease with which Utah was taken was partly because the defending troops lacked motorised transport and were using captured French, Soviet and Czech equipment. Many of the men were non-German conscripts, taken from Soviet and Polish prisoners of war. In all, the defending troops on this part of the landing beaches numbered 7000.

Nowadays, Utah Beach is a silent and windswept place of distant but still fiercely strong memories. We visited it first on the 50th anniversary of the landings, and this was my reaction:

The ranks of barbed wire and wicked metal stakes have long since gone, and the abandoned gun emplacements now lay mostly buried in the bone white sand. But surrounding the museum and memorial, a number of strangely archaic-looking engines of war lay scattered amongst the shallow dunes. Rather than being restored and scrupulously maintained as would happen in Britain, the rusting tanks and cannon appear to have been left where and as they were immediately after the battle, which seems somehow much more fitting as a stark example of what horrors happened here in relatively recent times.

From the car park we walked up to the brow and looked out at the calm waters, trying to imagine what it must have been like for both armies as the time for engagement drew near. Beyond the horizon, hundreds of tiny landing craft would be bouncing across the waves, carrying fearful and sometimes terror-struck young Americans, some of whom would never before have travelled a hundred miles from their homes or even seen the sea. After five miserable days crossing the Atlantic on a troop ship, they would have been confined to a muddy, rain soaked camp near the English coast, waiting for the order which would send them to fight and perhaps die in someone else's war. Then, when the order came, they would have spent endless hours tossed around on the grey and heaving waters of the English Channel, far from home, desperately weary, seasick and fearful as the moment to scramble ashore under a hail of fire approached. For many, death must have been almost a release.

On the shore and awaiting the invasion would not be a crack division of battle-hardened stormtroopers, but a makeshift army of young and elderly conscripts, summoned to kill people with whom they had no quarrel.

On this peaceful summer's day, I stood on the remains of a pill-box and tried to think how someone like my son would feel to be here, wearing a rough and ill-fitting uniform, clutching his rifle with a pounding heart and dry mouth, and trying not to show his terror as the sky became black with warplanes and the greatest armada in history rose slowly over the horizon. Then would come the hell of noise and screaming and explosion, with fear spurring inhumanities beyond the imaginings of those who have never had to fight for their lives.

With my privileged life and limited imagination, it was, of course, impossible to begin to appreciate what it would be like to have to risk leaving your life upon a distant beach so that other people might be free. Even so, it is a debt that our and future generations will never be able to repay, and should never forget.

*French Letters*

---

# Carentan

The Cotentin *marais* is a vast swathe of marshlands which almost bisects the peninsula.

It can be a magical place at any time of year, from the early months when it becomes a great inland sea to the summertime when cows graze upon the rich grasslands. Then will come the winter wonderland, when all is white with frost and the thousands of streams and rivulets freeze over and fall silent.

Carentan is an unassuming little town of 6000 residents lying between the *marais* and the sea and on the shoulder of the peninsula close to the border with Calvados. The town is on the site of an ancient Gallic port and at the confluence of three rivers. Together, they feed the Haut Dick canal, where battered scows and workmanlike boats rub shoulders with visiting yachts. The canal leads to a lock gate and, when the tide is right, the open waters beyond. In between times it is a shining, smooth wasteland of mud, relieved by fields of tall and slender reeds. A curiosity and constant fascination for us is that the canal runs over rather than under the busy RN13. To chug contentedly over tons of screaming metal is to underline just how pleasant travelling by inland waterways can be.

Another key location for the D-Day assaults, Carentan is known to millions around the world from TV series like *Band of Brothers*, and a number of computer games like *Call of Duty*.

A hamlet outside Carentan was where we found our third home on the peninsula. *Le Marais* was a gaunt, stone building of considerable size, looking out over hundreds of acres of marshlands. It had three sets of stairs and such a confusing layout that the removal men got lost twice and put the bedroom furniture in a sitting room, and the bathroom accessories in the kitchen.

Our plan was to convert the outhouses into different sorts of accommodation, and the barn into a huge dining and meeting place. Then we would set up a residential writing school. Guests would pay an all-in fee for a week at *Le Marais*. Each morning we would meet to talk about an aspect of the arts and crafts of creative writing, then the guests would work on a themed exercise before being free to explore the area. In the evenings we would gather in the Great Hall (the converted barn) for dinner and then a review of the embryo writers' work. All of this was discussed and planned down to the finest detail, but in a later book I explained how I had neglected to check out any broader considerations:

---

Our first day at our new home, and dawn is nigh. We watch contentedly as the eastern horizon begins to glow like the skin of an English tourist in southern France during high summer.

A train moves silently along the edge of the marshlands on its way to Paris and work, pleasure or sadness for those who travel in it. Nearer the house, a solitary tree appears through the retreating gloom, and a low whinny and snuffle breaks the silence. It has been a dry start to autumn, so cattle and horses still graze upon the plain. But in February, we shall be looking out across a huge lake.

The owls on the *marais* make their closing exchanges before they and the night depart, and a security lamp in the back yard of the house next door flashes on. Caught in the pool of light, a fox strolls across the flagstones, then pauses to look incuriously up at us. At my side I feel Milly bristle, and a low growl precedes a throaty bark of warning to the trespasser. I reach down and tap her muzzle lightly to remind her that we now have neighbours to consider.

Then, all hell breaks loose.

The air is rent with a cacophony of yelping, baying and barking, and it is as if at least two packs of hounds have arrived to compete over which should have the pleasure of ripping the fox to shreds. Milly cowers into a corner, then we hear a distant shout and the bedlam abates almost as quickly as it erupted.

I totter to the balcony wall and look numbly into the gloom. The explosion of noise seems to have come from a large barn close by the fence marking the start of our neighbour's land. It is no more than a hundred feet from the main house and planned guest accommodation.

My wife and I stare at each other as silence returns, then I realise the awful truth. After years of warning readers of the potential hazards of buying property in France and stressing the importance of location above virtually all other virtues, I appear to have bought us a house next door to an obviously thriving dog kennels.

*French Lessons*

---

# Saint-Lô

Although Saint-Lô bows to Cherbourg in terms of size and population, it is the prefecture or administrative 'capital' of the department.

If it had one, even its mother would not think of Saint-Lô as attractive. Curiously, the reason for the lack of visual appeal won the town a very signal honour. Such was the near-total destruction after the D-Day Landings, Saint-Lô is what became known as a 'martyr city' of World War II. As Malta received the George Cross from Britain, Saint-Lô was awarded the *Legion d'Honneur* in 1948.

A strategic crossroads, the town was occupied by the Germans in 1940, and in the Liberation Saint-Lô had the dubious distinction of being bombed by both sides. On the night of the 6th of June, there was a heavy bombardment by American forces. During the Battle of Saint-Lô on the 17th, the town was attacked by German bombers, and then by American planes as part of *Operation Cobra. It is estimated that more than 97 percent of the town was destroyed, earning it the grim title of 'Capital of the ruins' in a work by Irish playwright Samuel Becket. As one American GI was said to have said after the dust had finally settled: 'We sure liberated the hell out of that town...'

Following the Liberation, there were suggestions that Saint-Lô be left in ruins as a stark reminder of the savagery and folly of war. But the remaining members of the community voted to restore their town, or try to. Unfortunately, the restoration took place when the dominant design style chosen was known as neo-functionalism and executed in mostly rough-cast concrete. It looks as awful as it sounds, and one can only imagine what the first city of Manche would have looked like in its historic pre-war splendour.

*Operation Cobra was the code name for the massive 'clean-up' operation launched by the US army seven weeks after D-Day. The idea was to punch through the German lines penning in

*Allied troops and allow them to advance into Brittany. Significant engagements on the peninsula are marked by curious monuments with a strange resemblance to a brightly-painted Dalek.*

## Villedieu-les-Poêles

After Saint-Lô, Villedieu-Les-Poêles seems a completely different kettle of fish. Were it a real fish kettle, it would probably be made of copper and up for sale at a saw-you-coming tourist price.

Whereas Saint-Lô is all about concrete and administration, Villedieu is all about age, tourism and copper souvenirs, but in a non-offensive way.

The town has long been associated with the manufacture of posh pots and pans, which is where the hyphenated bit of the name originates. Confusingly, 'poêle' can mean a stove or the pot or pan. So you can have a wood-burning poêle with a crêpe poêle sitting on top of it.

The road to becoming a renowned centre of coppersmithing is an interesting one and began in the 12th century when Henry I of England (also the Duke of Normandy) gifted Villedieu to the religious order which was to become the Knights of Malta. It is thought probably that the Knights imported craftsmen with advanced skills in using copper into the town, and by the 14th century the Corporation of Coppersmiths of Villedieu was recognised and admired throughout France.

By the end of the 18th century, the town had also become renowned for the manufacture of large church bells. The constant din of them being made and tested together with the banging away at copper pots and pans all day resulted in the nickname for all residents of Villedieu of *sourdins*, which means - in this context- 'deaf ones'.

Equally interesting is how the town escaped any significant damage in the Liberation. As the Germans withdrew from the town, they left behind a sniper who accounted for several American soldiers. After he was taken care of, the US commander was about to order a bombing run on the town when the mayor arrived to reassure him there was not a single enemy left in Villedieu. He offered to sit in the front seat of a jeep and tour the town to prove it, and his brave intervention meant that Villedieu-Les-Poêles still has such a wealth of beautiful old buildings.

# Le Mont Saint-Michel

Mont-St-Michel is in the top ten in the charts of the most popular tourist destinations in the country.

That is saying something when you think of how many highly visitable places there are in France. Even more impressive is the fact that the little island is only beaten by Paris-based attractions like the Eiffel Tower and the Louvre museum. This popularity pleases the Normans, but not the Bretons, who think it should belong to them.

People confuse the two, but the 'Mont' refers to the isle on which the Gothic-style Benedictine Abbey sits. The isle is no more than a kilometre from the shore and 247 acres (100 hectares) in surface area. The permanent population is only 44, but coming up for three million pilgrims and tourists visit the 'Pyramid of the Sea' each year. Given the few days a year that the isle is closed to the public, that's something like eight thousand visitors every single day.

According to legend, the Archangel for whom the isle is named appeared to the bishop of nearby Avranches in 708 and instructed him to build a church on the rocky islet. The bishop (St Aubert) repeatedly ignored the heavenly command until he was persuaded by an angelic finger burning a hole in his skull.

The ownership of the isle has been disputed for more than a millennium, and the first change of hands came in 867. The King of the Franks finding himself unable to defend his territory from the Vikings, granted the whole Cotentin peninsula and the island to Brittany, who felt they could do a better job. Apparently not so, as In 993 the notorious William Longsword annexed the peninsula in the name of Normandy.

There is still a degree of (mostly) good-natured dispute because Mont-St-Michel stands at the mouth of the river Couesnon, which was traditionally reckoned to mark the boundary between the two regions. Bretons say that the river has changed course over the centuries, which is why it now appears to be on the Norman side of the border, and should come back to them. Locals scoff at that claim and say the border was never the river, anyway.

Whoever it belongs to, it is a truly awe-inspiring sight which we have driven, ridden, walked, sailed and even swam past on many occasions. We joined the masses crossing the causeway once, and immediately saw further attractions. The island is not just about the abbey; it is an almost perfectly preserved medieval village. Admission charges are most reasonable, and a visit highly recommended.

Mont St Michel is a landmark visible from miles around, and rises from the bay like a computer-generated image in a modern movie about a time that never was. It would be a shame to admire it only from a distance, and no visit to Normandy is really complete unless you have come into close contact with the Pyramid of the Sea.

## Avranches

We have stayed, lived in or passed through hundreds of French towns. As with human beings, sometimes one likes them on sight, and sometimes the opposite. There doesn't have to be a reason for this first impression, but we liked Avranches immediately we arrived.

It may be that its population of 8000 makes it a big-small town with lots going on, or the floral gardens that give it the air of a sedate English seaside resort. It might be the centrepiece of the ancient castle it might even be the fascination of the skull of St Aubert, complete with angelic hole, which is on show at the Basilica of St Gervase.

Whatever it is, we are in good company for finding the town so appealing. In his novel *Notre Couer*, the master wordsmith Guy de Maupassant had this to say about Avranches:

*The houses crowning the heights gave to the place from a distance the appearance of a fortification. Seen close at hand, it was an ancient and pretty Norman city, with small dwellings of regular and almost similar appearance built closely adjoining one another, giving an aspect of ancient pride and modern comfort, a feudal yet peasant-like air.*

Our first visit to this pretty Norman town came in 1994, when we escorted a D-Day veteran on his first return to where he had come ashore. Or where he thought he had come ashore.

Reg was a potman at our favourite pub in Portsmouth. He did a daily bit of cleaning and glass-clearing, and the landlord kept him on out of respect and not pity. Reg was one of those veterans who really did not like to talk about his wartime service, but mentioned one evening he would like to visit Normandy before it was too late. He had never been more than a private, but a kindly former Marine Colonel loaned us his beret and badge. This forgiveable subterfuge guaranteed Reg access to all areas for the various events, and at one ceremony he found himself seated in the VIP stand within touching distance of the President of France.

Over the three days, our old friend was treated with the utmost courtesy and respect by dignitaries and *gendarmerie*, and got through at least a bottle of scotch a day at the official and unofficial functions. When we asked where he had landed, he said he thought it was Avranches but when we said there were no landings there he admitted it could well have been Arromanches.

What the former Royal Marine bandsman did remember vividly half a century on was asking a sergeant in the landing craft what he should do when they got ashore. Knowing that Reg as a RM bandsman was more familiar with using a pair of drumsticks than a Lee Enfield 303, the man said he should just keep his head down and shoot at the blokes with funny-shaped helmets.

Looking back into his distant past as we prepared for another toast, the old soldier said it was not until some time after the landings that he realised that the German helmets were not that different in shape from the ones his American allies were wearing...

# Granville

If Avranches is the Bognor or Bournemouth of this part of the Cotentin coastline, Granville must be the Brighton.

I first visited the then not-nearly-so-trendy resort in the 1990s in my role as editor of a food and drink magazine. My mission was to review an award-winning restaurant and hotel, recently taken over by a former chef at Maxim's of Paris. I had taken on the arduous journey out of sympathy to our proper food critic as he had never taken a ferry boat to France and might well, I managed to convince him, fall prey to the horrors of seasickness with no escape for six hours.

I still remember the meal, which was marked by its heavenly simplicity. The main course was sea bream, and it almost literally melted in my mouth. When I asked the chef how he had prepared and cooked it and what was his secret, he looked at me as if I had asked a stupid question. He then gave a force five Gallic shrug and said he had done little more than take the fish from the sea, wrap it up and put it in the oven. It was the quality and freshness of the fish and the way it was prepared and cooked quickly and simply that was the secret.

There are now many more award-winning hotels and restaurants in Granville, which has become a very upmarket resort, with my comparison with Brighton based on the distinct odour of money overcoming the tang of the ozone.

Granville sits on a headland with wonderful sea views and walks along the rugged coastline, and there is a striking citadel which once guarded that part of the coast. But it is the beach resort which sums up the town for me. The broad stretch of manicured sands is backed with rows of pristine white beach huts, and on the hill above stands a gloriously pink villa which looks as if it must have once belonged to someone who liked to catch the public eye and attention.

In fact, it was the childhood home of legendary fashion designer Christian Dior. The villa is now a museum dedicated to the great man, and also regularly stages the haughtiest of *haute couture* exhibitions.

Other attractions include the *Haut Ville* - a lofty collection of ramparts, grand buildings and restaurants - and an absolute abundance of very stylish and expensive chocolate, knick-knack and gourmet grocery shops. No sticks of rock with 'Granville' running through them that I could find, though.

As with our last visit, the in-your-face high-endedness was too rich for our simple tastes and shallow pockets, but I can see the appeal to those with the money and the inclination to spend it.

## Coutances

Although destroyed by Vikings in 866 and then knocked about a bit at regular intervals until and including the Liberation, Coutances has a feel of uninterrupted and largely serene history.

The undoubted star of the elevated town and perhaps the main contributor to its feeling of permanence and tranquility is the remarkable twin-towered 13th-century cathedral. Its clean vertical lines soaring to a height of nearly 300 hundred feet make it an icon for lovers of the Gothic style, and it can actually be seen from the Island of Jersey on clear days.

The *Cathédrale de Notre-Dame de Coutances* has some stunning stained glass windows, a number of which have somehow survived through the turbulence of more than seven centuries. A particularly absorbing couple of panels feature the lives and grisly fates of the saints George and Thomas Becket.

For this and other reasons I could not put my finger on, Coutances has the feel of a sophisticated county town, and has won several awards just for being itself.

There are plenty of ancient buildings which survived the Liberation, and the Old Town has an eye-pleasing network of courtyards and narrow streets. There is an unusual and permanent exhibition of Norman ceramics at the museum, which also features work by a number of 20th-century artists from the town and surrounding areas.

Another popular feature is an annual festival satisfyingly called Jazz under the Apple Trees, and overall, Coutances is very much a place to relax in, though also a tailor-made base for walking, hiking, mountain biking and cycling or other energetic exercises.

# Sea Bream en papillote

'En papillote' means 'in parchment' but nowadays the French like to use modern substitutes. A friend in Normandy always swore that the sports pages of the regional newspaper were best when he was cooking trout for us after a day at the local *étang de péche*.

This is, I believe, more or less how the chef at Granville cooked our sea bream, but the formula and method work equally well with other types of fish and certainly helps the flesh fall off the bone and melt in the mouth. This version takes no more than half an hour and feeds a hungry couple.

## Ingredients

One very fresh sea bream of about 500g, *gutted, washed and patted dry
A handful of new potatoes, sliced to the thickness of a pound coin.
A good dash of cider
A good dash of Calvados
Some olive oil
Some seasoning
A lemon
Some sprigs of rosemary

## Method

Preheat your oven to 200$^0$C.
Boil the new potatoes until tender but not fully cooked (usually about five or six minutes). Drain and leave them while you prepare the fish.
Score the skin of the fish at intervals of around 3cm.
Rub the Calvados into the fish inside and out.
Season all over, inside and out.
Stuff the cavity with some slices of lemon and some rosemary.

Repeat the process on the upper outside of the fish, putting rosemary into the slashes and covering with lemon rings.

Oil a suitably large piece of parchment paper (or the sports pages of the Normandy edition of *Ouest France*).

Lay the potatoes on the paper so they make a platform for the fish.

Make a tightly fitting package, leaving one end open.

Pour a little cider (about 30 ml) into the open end, then seal the package.

Cook for no more than a half hour.

Serve with suitable accompaniment/s

*Your first time gutting and cleaning a fish is always a bit daunting, but simpler than it sounds. You will need a sharp knife and a chopping board to hand, and start by grasping the fish by the tail and scraping the scales 'against the grain', beginning at the tail and continuing till they are all gone. Then lay the fish on the cutting board and make a cut along the belly from head to tail. Remove all the guts, then scrape the inside cavity clean. If you are going to leave the head on, cut the gills off.*

*Cut off the tail if you must. Now rinse the inside and out under a fast-flowing tap. Pat the fish dry inside and out with a suitable cloth and you are good to go.*

## Créances

As previously discussed, the Normans will form an appreciation society for almost any dish from rice pudding to tripe. In the town which is next on our itinerary, they like to celebrate a culinary raw material, and have a festival and fair to so do. Here is what I wrote on our first visit to what is an unusual event even for rural Normandy:

---

Créances is a small town on the west coast of the Cotentin peninsula, and is known throughout the region for its carrots.

Normans, like most other French people I have met are not particularly enthusiastic about vegetables, but are fiercely proud - also like most other French people I know- of any regional claims to singularity.

Residents of this part of the Cotentin claim the highest cliffs in Europe, some of the most interesting (i.e. changeable) weather in the country, and inarguably, the biggest, reddest and most succulent carrots in all France. The fine and sandy soil of the miles of flat coastline on this side of the peninsula is an ideal breeding ground for certain vegetables, and Créances is proud to be the carrot capital of the Cotentin.

Other towns in our region compete to have the finest floral or artistic arrangements marking their boundaries, but on the roundabout outside this town, pride of place goes to an ornate carrot mosaic. It is now the time of year which brings the commune an excuse to show off their claim to fame. The early crop has just been pulled, and for the next two days Créances will abandon itself to a near-orgy of celebration and self-congratulation. During the festival, tens of thousands of visitors will throng the streets and marvel at the wealth and variety of uses for the town's signature vegetable.

At dozens of stalls lining the square, visitors will be able to sample and buy carrot-flavoured cake, bread, terrine, soup, wine and calvados. At some stalls they will even be able to buy carrots in their natural state. Many artists and craftsmen will have taken on the challenge of working with the most common local material, and there will be sometimes breathtaking examples of their arts and skills. There will be intricately carved miniature sculptures of birds, animals and buildings, and minutely detailed representations of historical characters and events. Last year, the visitors marvelled at a complete representation of the storming of the Bastille crafted entirely from carrots. At other times I have seen chess sets and small items of jewellery fashioned from the town's premier product. One year there was even an attempt to hold a fashion parade of *haute couture* clothing made entirely from carrot peelings, but it was not a success.

*French Lessons*

---

# Lessay

As Créances has its *Fête de la Carotte*, our next port of call has its long-serving horse fair, and it is one of the biggest and probably the longest established affairs in the Cotentin calendar.

For the rest of the year, Lessay is another unassuming small town in the heart of the peninsula, primarily distinguished by being the location of a 10th-century monastery which is agreed to be one of the finest examples of Romanesque (medieval European) architecture in the region.

But it all changes for the Sainte-Croix Fair. The event is nearly as old as the monastery and takes place in the second week of September. The whole town is taken over, with 42 acres (17 hectares) transformed into one enormous market. Over the three days, more than 400,000 people will arrive to join in the fun. When you think that is more than the entire population of the peninsula, you can see what a draw it is.

The Fair is a mecca for horse-lovers, and a predictable stop-off and annual meeting place for travelling people. There is a permanent encampment on the outskirts, and for the Fair it becomes the biggest gypsy settlement in Europe.

If comparisons were possible, I would say the Sainte-Croix is not so much a typical French *fête* or *foire* as a really big county show in England. The bare statistics tell the story and during just one day, there will be more than a thousand horses, ponies and donkeys changing hands. On another day, 300 sheep and goats will be traded. While this is happening, there will be dog, poultry and livestock shows, and the more than 1500 exhibitors will include fifty wine merchants and twenty gourmet food wholesalers. There are also lashings of imaginative attractions for the children, like ghost trains, an ice palace, a big wheel, quad bike riding and something intriguingly called Barracks Shooting.

Then there's all the stands and tents trying to cope with the demand for food and drink. It is said in the peninsula that if you can't sell what you want to sell at Lessay, you should give up being a salesman.

Keeping order at the fair will be no more than a hundred or so policemen and four Republican Guards on horseback. Most of them will have no more arduous or dangerous duties than sampling the goods and sending those few cars not heading for the show on a diversion round the town.

## Port-Bail

If towns could be compared with steak, Port-Bail would perhaps be a *filet mignon*. Small and sweet and appetising to look at. Or rather, the bit sitting on the shore is small and sweet and tasty-looking. Like most old fishing villages, Port-Bail is a town of two halves, though even the top end away from the water has a pleasing durability and lack of modernity about it.

When we were working on our second second-home in the Cotentin, we would keep going until late evening, then abandon the cement mixer and speed to Port-Bail for a meal. *The Rendez vous des Pecheurs* was a favourite of sailors from Jersey, who would come and go according to tides so kept odd hours, and the restaurant would stay open late to accommodate them. To serve food after eight in the evening even in the height of summer was considered an almost degenerate practice by other restaurateurs in those days. But the staff never raised an eyebrow when we heaved to at nine or even later. We liked sitting upstairs, sometimes in our cement and paint-laden working clothes, and watching the sun settle on the horizon while we tucked into vats of mussels which had travelled no further than the hundred yards to the kitchen door from the water's edge.

Above all, what we loved about Port-Bail and so many fishing ports and villages was how it lived beside and from the sea. Before having homes in rural France, we had never lived more than a mile from the sea. This was not because we were rich, but because nowhere in the small island city of Portsmouth is more than a mile from the water's edge. We bought the Little Jewel and other homes in the heart of the countryside because we would not have been able to so do in Britain at a price we could afford to pay. But the sea is and will stay in our blood, so a visit to the coast a couple of times a week to top up on the salty sights and smells and ambience was in our rules-of-living book.

Port-Bail was more or less just down the road in French terms from our farmhouse, and suited us perfectly. The weekly market seemed somehow more special because you could buy the fiery Norman version of a hot dog in sight, sound and smell of the water, and eat it sitting by the old church on the shore, looking out across the long causeway to where the boats bobbed and curtsied prettily. The reason the causeway is so long is to match the tide, which makes the exposed area of sand and mud and seamarsh a place of rich pickings for seafood gatherers.

The last time we were here was nearly twenty years ago, and we are delighted to find that not much had changed.

The nice thing about communities on a shore stuffed with eye-pleasing old buildings is that they usually cannot be messed about with. Developers can't build out over the sea (yet) and there is usually not a foot of spare space in the typically tightly-huddled fishing village. Even if it were possible, only a madman would pay the price to buy a whole terrace of ancient cottages lining a quay and replace them with a block of luxury apartments. Having said that, that is exactly what is happening where the developers can get around the rules and throw money at the owners of the properties getting in the way of their ambitions.

On second thoughts, perhaps the analogy with a *filet-mignon* is not, as my French friends might say, *juste*. Port-Bail is small and nice, but not at all pretentious, overvalued and bum-clenchingly expensive. Perhaps I should compare it rather with those monster bowls of scrumptious mussels we would so often enjoy there all those years ago.

# Barneville-Carteret

Continuing our clockwise tour of the west coast, we have arrived at two towns with only a hyphen between them in distance as well as title. The feel and presentation of each are, however, quite distinct - or seem so to us.

Barneville-Carteret is a commune of a little more than 2000, and the two villages married and became one in 1964 after a long courtship.

I do not know why, but Barneville always seemed to have a more homely and almost bucket-and-spade appeal, while Carteret was clearly aiming for the high end of the tourist trade. It is at Carteret you will find the magnificent hotels perched on the quayside and looking out towards Jersey. There is also a cluster of restaurants which sport gleaming white linen tablecloths, always a clue to the likely price per head. Years ago we ate at one with napkins shaped like swans, and the bill for four came to £200. Luckily I was being treated by a now-defunct ferry company, and I often wondered if the cost of that meal hastened their demise. Fifty quid a head might not sound extortionate, but this was twenty years ago. I should imagine you have to pay to look in the window nowadays.

Though Carteret has long been reckoned to be a pretty swish place, there was the odd not-so-sophisticated eaterie. Below is a description of a memorable meal, and please note that the restaurant no longer exists:

To Carteret and a special treat for our Italian house guests.

Known elsewhere and somewhat ironically as the St Tropez of Cotentin, Carteret is a former fishing village on the west coast which now boasts more restaurants, bistros and bars per head than any other settlement on the peninsula. One is an interesting Italian-style restaurant which is owned by a barking mad patron who seems at permanent odds with his live-in waitress and lover.

On our first visit there, crockery exploded off stage in the kitchen before he fled into the night, leaving customers to rescue their own pizzas from the oven. There followed a series of dramatic phone calls, causing the girlfriend to desert us in mid-serve and follow him into the street before both returned for a tearful reunion at the next table.

Thinking this will all make Rinaldo feel at home, we arrive for the matinee performance and study the menu. Our friend is not amused to find that the only wine on offer is French, which he takes as a comment on the standing of his own country's produce.

After letting off a fruitless burst of Italian at the waitress, he demands to see the owner, and is even more upset to find that he too is French, and that he learned his art and craft when working as a delivery biker for the famous *Pizza Tout d'Suite* Takeaway in Cherbourg.

The meal goes from bad to worse, as Rinaldo is duly surprised and extremely unhappy to find a French cheese topping on his Neapolitan Surprise Special, and the final straw is the discovery that the English translation of the desserts on offer includes his alleged regional speciality, Banana Shit.

*René & Me*

_____

# Flamanville

Flamanville is notable for its wonderfully over-the-top moated château, which is all soaring spires, witch-hat pointy towers and crenellated battlements.

This is the part of the west coast which claims the tallest cliffs in Normandy if not Europe, and here there's a former signal station which offers fabulous views across to what we call the Channel Islands and the French grudgingly concede as the *Isles Anglo-Normandes*.

There is what is said to be a very, very good restaurant here; the seafood and other menu items at *La Sémaphore* find favour in the Michelin Guide. There is a special mention for the owner, who is apparently a font of knowledge about the area.

Since 1985, though, I think it would be fair to say that Flamanville has mostly been associated with the nearby nuclear power plant. In 2005, it generated four percent of the power used for the whole of France, which is impressive if not particularly pleasing to the people in whose back yards it was built. There have also been various safety scares and concerns about the dangers of flooding. Construction of a new reactor began at the end of 2007, with a completion date of 2012 and a budget or 3.3 billion Euros. The current estimate is a completion date at the end of 2018, and a revised budget of more than 10.5 billion.

Whenever it is finished and whatever it costs, I hope the security is better than when we made an unscheduled visit.

It was the beginning of the 90s, and we were working our way along the coastal road to see if we could find an affordable place with a view across the sea. We were both on the lookout for any *A Vendre* (For Sale) signs, so were suprised to find ourselves in a queue of cars. Even more surprising, they were waiting at that most unusual of devices in this part of the peninsula, a set of traffic lights. It was not until they turned green that I realised the vehicles in front were turning off the road and through a gateway in a very high and substantial metal fence, topped with rolls of lethal-looking razor wire.

It was also a little unnerving to see that two large persons in blue outfits obviously modelled on *Gendarmerie* uniforms were standing on either side of the gate and casting an eye over each vehicle and its driver before waving them through. Even more unnerving was that they both cradled automatic weapons. It is not unusual to see people in uniform with guns in France, but it occurred to me that the men must be guarding something more security-worthy than a yoghurt factory with a secret recipe to protect.

As I wound down the window of our clearly foreign (i.e. right-hand drive with British number plates) car, the guard on my wife's side glanced through the windscreen, smiled at her and waved us through. It was then that I saw the Radiation Hazard symbol on a large building in front of us, and realised we were definitely not on the premises of a yoghurt factory.

My suspicions were confirmed by the wail of sirens and the strobing of flashing blue lights as two cars overtook us and pulled in front, issuing at least four men with even bigger and nasty-looking weapons than those at the gate.

Strangely, it took no more than a few minutes for us to convince the senior officer that we were British tourists looking for the château and not terrorists, and we were escorted off the premises.

As my wife observed when I drove somewhat shakily away, if there were any gangs with evil intent to the nuclear plant, they could do no better than pose as two middle-aged and not very bright Britons with a really old Volvo estate car.

## Biville

There is a Biville-sur-Mer in Upper Normandy, but the Cotentin version is a little smaller and for us more pleasingly homely. The village and area has a long history, and there is much more to Biville than might first meet the eye. Before a modern road development brushed them aside, here there were burial mounds dating back to the Bronze age, and a trove of Roman coins has been unearthed across the years.

There is inevitable dispute as to the origin of the name, with some proponents for Ancient Norse, and others that it stems from the name of a long-ago liege lord. There is certainly an interesting Spanish connection in the form of a town of the same name in Galicia, standing alongside on the road to St Jacques de Compestella. As one of the pilgrim routes from England passed this way, there is speculation that the Spanish town may have been named for the Cotentin one.

More religious connections in that the village has its own saint, who was said to have miraculously protected the refugees trying to escape a plague that ravaged Cherbourg in 1630.

Biville was also the setting for the cliff-top cottage with stunning sea views that we fell for before we stumbled on the Mill of the Flea. Below is the reason we did not put in an offer:

---

The pretty whitewashed and red-tiled-roofed fisherman's cottage sat close but not too close to the cliff edge. It was not many miles from the nuclear power plant, but as the estate agent said with an eloquent shrug, if the *atomique* were to go up it would take most of the peninsula with it, so proximity was hardly an issue.

There was a level garden alongside the property which would make a perfect place to sit and look out across the bay while having dinner or a drink as dusk fell. In short, it was pretty near perfect, but there was a snag.

The room with the best view across the bay was an extension on the seaward side of the cottage. The problem was that it didn't go with the rest of the property.

According to the local *notaire*, the neighbour who owned the extension had declared most vehemently he would never, ever sell it, and any future buyers would not be allowed to use it. This even though the room had lain empty and unused for years and he had never taken up his right to visit or occupy it.

His attitude, the agent suggested, probably stemmed from the fact that an almost identical extension on his property was actually owned by the proprietor of the cottage we wanted to buy.

In a simpler world, he sighed, the owners of each property would have agreed to swap their foreign possessions, and everybody would be happy.

But as he said with an even more shoulder-hiking shrug, property exchange in France was never, ever that simple…

*Home & Dry in France*

_____

# Vauville

I love this part of the peninsula. But then I love all parts of the Cotentin, and the variety of the landscape is just one reason. At the start of our journey through Lower Normandy we were walking and cycling along the flat, sandy beaches of the east coast, then driving through miles of tiny tree-lined fields in the *bocage*. Now we are in a windswept place of moorland and gaunt cliffs, endlessly besieged by the crashing waves of the Celtic Sea. This makes it even stranger to find ourselves in a world of palm trees and exotic plants.

Many places in France claim to have 'micro-climates' which are far superior to areas even relatively just down the road. It is said that the conjunction of natural features and tides have created an oasis here. I don't know if that is a serious or sustainable claim, but it is certainly true that the Botanical Gardens at Vauville evoke a feeling of being in a far more exotic part of the world. This is even more remarkable as the garden is only a few hundred yards from the Atlantic Ocean.

Surrounding a particularly impressive château, the garden was laid down in 1948 and contains nearly a thousand examples of semi-tropical plants and trees, cunningly protected by windbreaks.

*Normandy is defined by its bocage – or the way the pastureland is often divided up into small fields, each lined with deciduous trees. The fields are often banked high above the country roads and lanes, which made it difficult and often very costly for the Allies to make progress during the Liberation.*

It is strange how we have given birds human characteristics. We see the eagle as majestic and the owl wise, the sparrow chirpy and cheeky, and the crow opportunistic and cunning. The puffin is regarded as a friendly and inoffensive type and almost a clown.

The *fratercula artica* is known more familiarly as the sea parrot, and its impressive beak shows why. One of their favourite habitats is the boulders at the bottom of steep cliffs, so this part of the peninsula is as good as it gets if you are a puffin looking for a home. We first saw the colony here after a good lunch, and I thought they were penguins until an exasperated twitcher put me right.

Puffin-watching is a treat which is becoming rarer, due to a number of factors. One is the human overfishing of stocks of sand eel and whitebait, and another is climate change. Such is the decline that puffins were this year declared by the IUCN (International Union for Conservation and Nature) a threatened species. Another good reason for coming to the Cotentin to see them in their rugged but enchanting habitat.

## Nez de Jobourg, Auderville

Part of the *Armorican Massif* of ancient rock running through the north-west of France and Brittany, the *Nez* or Nose of Jobourg juts out into an often wild and dangerous sea. Shags, fulmars and herring gulls wheel and screech overhead, and more than a hundred metres below lie caves imbued with tales of mystery and legend. There's the Fairy Hole and the Lion Cave, and even two grottos disguising a route from shore to town for smugglers. It is very similar to Cornwall here, with - some people might say - the added advantage of being in France.

Auderville is the end of the road in this corner of the peninsula, and leads to what is known in tourist-speak as the Lighthouse at the End of the World. The Raz Blanchard earned its name from the white frill of waves resulting from one of the strongest tidal currents in the world.

In 1823, seven ships sank off la Hague and the project to site a lighthouse at Cape Goury was begun. After fierce struggles with the weather, the granite tower was completed in 1837 and helped reduce the carnage off the rocky shores. The light went out when the Germans arrived, but was switched on again when it was liberated on the 1st of July 1944.

It grows dusk and we must look for a convenient parking place for Dodo the Tardis. Tomorrow we will reach the end of our most sentimental of journeys by returning to the places and people which stole our hearts all those years ago.

# Bricquebec

When we left the Little Jewel we did not have to travel far to our new home.

After frantically rushing to every part of the peninsula to look at places which fell short in one way or another, we exchanged misty-eyed looks and put in an on-the-spot offer on the old farmhouse and ruined mill no more than a dozen miles from Valognes.

Although it was not part of our considerations, the location of La Puce was just about perfect for us. On the edge of ancient marshland and rich with folklore, history and families which had lived in the same villages and homes for generations, this part of the peninsula was certainly intriguing in all sorts of ways. In one direction was a small town with an eccentric character running a bar awash with eccentric customers. In the other direction was a bigger town with an eccentric character running a bar awash with eccentric customers. In between was an age-old village on the edge of the *marais*, allegedly home to wizards, witches, a man who had been on first name terms with Willliam the Conqueror - and with a grocery shop and bar run by a woman to be truly reckoned with.

There is an old saying in this part of the Cotentin that all roads lead to Bricquebec. As with Rome, this is not meant as a statement of fact, but a measure of the local importance of the ancient market town. It really is at the centre of the lives of many tens of thousands of country people, who are naturally proud of its history and singularities. One of the claims to fame is that the square in Bricquebec is the largest in all Normandy. Another is that a cavalcade of dignitaries from Good Queen Bess to President Mitterand on a dirty weekend have stayed in the hotel in the grounds of the castle.

Whether those claims are strictly or remotely accurate, it is true that successive Dukes of Normandy looked upon Bricquebec as an important stronghold, and the castle makes that clear. Most of the soaring walls of the castle remain and are kept in good shape by commune and department. One entrance looks out onto the square, while the other is guarded by the lofty *donjon*.

*(Info-note: In France, what we know as a dungeon is an oubliette from the verb 'to forget.' A donjon is a keep or guard tower.)*

Regardless of whether it is the largest in all Normandy, the square at Bricquebec is an impressive size, and adequately surrounded by bars and restaurants. Our local for the 13 years we lived at La Puce was the *Café de Paris*, overseen by Freddo and his lovely wife Collette. Still there on permanent broom duty and to castigate the customers was Freddo's mother-in-law, the only person I saw him defer to. When we were there, the redoubtable *Maman* was a living link with the past, having served drinks to and rebutted the advances of German soldiers in the War years.

Perhaps because of her presence and Freddo's approach to service levels and elastic opening times - the *Cafe de Paris* still held that feeling of a bang-on traditional bar favoured by generations of thirsty customers.

Monday was the best day of the week for Freddo and the other bar owners, as it was when the market came to town. It was our delight to beat the crowds and take coffee with the owner of the most monumental moustache in town as he prepared for the rush, but found time to give us lessons in the local patois. Mostly, it has to be said, in the many ways of being rude to other road users:

---

It is not yet dawn, but we are already hard at work over coffee and *calva* in the *Café de Paris*.

In the barely aired streets two farmers squabble half-heartedly over the price of a bored ewe as they work themselves up for market day in Bricquebec.

Soon the sheep, pigs, calfs and cows will arrive in a convoy of trailers, lorries and vans, and in some cases even in the back of cars or towed behind mopeds and the serious business of the day will begin. After the stock has changed hands, the square will be hosed down and made ready for the stall holders, while the farmers will move to the bars to take a glass of wine or apple brandy and complain about how badly they have done, even - and often especially - when they have not.

But for now, the near-deserted square calmly awaits the arrival of the weekly circus, while a pair of rooks take their ease on the church tower, hoarsely discussing the possibilities of rich pickings when the day's trading is done.

This has been the way of things in Bricquebec for centuries, and is a very civilised way to start the day.

*René & Me*

# St Sauveur-le Vicomte

For most visitors, the nearest town to the Mill of the Flea is known for the remnants of its ancient castle and abbey. The castle has massive towers and the walls were breached by cannon during a siege in 1374. This was one of the first successful use of guns against castles.

Literary enthusiasts know that one of France's most respected authors lies in the shadow of the broached walls. Jules-Amédéé Barbey d'Aurevilly specialised in tales of mystery and imagination. He influenced the work of later and perhaps better-known writers like American writer Henry James and our long-winded Norman friend and madeleine cake fan Marcel Proust.

Barbey d'Aurevilly was a contradictory character, at the same time a staunch Catholic and dandy who wrote about sometimes risqué subjects. He was and is admired greatly in literary circles but I have never met anyone outside the town who knows of his work. His portrait shows a tall, lean and rather unhappy man. Perhaps he knew even then he was not going to be remembered in history a fraction as much as those he led along the path to great literature.

For hundreds of people in the town and area, St-Sauveur-le-Vicomte was known primarily for the simple but angelic traditional *midi* menu on offer at the little bar by the church, but perhaps even more so for the completely barking owner of *Le Rideau Cramoisi.*

Coco leCoq looked like nobody else I ever knew; the closest I could come would be a cross between the wild-eyed and haired professor in *Back to the Future*, and the bulbous-eyed Asterix the Gaul. Coco was a big man for a rural Norman in those days, with a mass of Viking-style red hair and drooping moustache that somehow emphasised his awful teeth when he smiled or laughed, which was often.

Coco was truly a force of nature, and at the same time a thoughtful man with a love of art. His wide shoulders and strong arms came from his artisanal approach to creativity, and from his penchant from digging up petrified tree trunks from the marais and sculpting them into abstract works of art. There was a weekly exhibition at his bar, at which all local artists were invited to display their work.

While Coco was the draw for drinkers who liked a landlord with character, those who came to his bar were mostly attracted by the rustic cooking of Coco's wife, Chantal.

Every Monday to Friday fifty seats would be up for grabs at the Flaming Curtains, and office workers in smart suits and posh expatriates would happily rub shoulders with overalled farm workers. Each lunchtime was a truly shared experience and celebration of superb Norman traditional cooking.

It was a rare winter's evening we did not drop into the Flaming Curtains to talk about life and admire Coco's latest creation. Best of all was when we would find him sitting on the flagstones in front of a roaring fire, pouring yet another bottle of rough cider into the cauldron which held the ham hocks which would be the main item on the next day's menu.

Coco also had a passion for all sorts of music and liked to promote international goodwill by arranging exchange concerts between similar groups of musicians from either side of the English Channel. Sometimes, however, a combination of strong drink and inattention cold lead to some interesting exchanges:

---

Yesterday we arrived at the Flaming Curtains to find Coco's latest exchange concert in full swing. Menacing-looking youths with shaven heads, Union Jack tee-shirts and lace-up boots gyrated happily in front of the church while a band advertised as the British Bulldogs performed on a makeshift stage.

When I asked him if he was sure that he had picked the right band for the sleepy town, he smiled and assured us that his customers were very fond of traditional English folk music.

Surprisingly, the bar and town remained unscathed, and all went so well that the band are booked for a return visit this summer.

Celebrating the success of the event, Coco told us he is negotiating for a visit of the St Sauveur abbey choir to a forthcoming London folk concert featuring the Bulldogs and fellow artistes *Die for England* and

*We Hate Fucking Foreigners.*

*René & Me*

---

*\*Le Rideau Cramoisi* ('The Crimson Curtain') was a short story by Barbey d'Aurevilly for which Coco's bar was named. Struggling for a translation, I came up with *The Flaming Curtains* and the name stuck with expat locals.

# Ham hock with apples, cider and mustard

I don't know if you have access to a cauldron, but this oven-cooked version is a close approximation to Coco LeCoq's winter signature dish:

## Ingredients

A good knob of goose fat
4 ham hocks
A clove of garlic
An onion
Four sweet apples
A pint (600 ml) of the roughest cider you can get
A glass of Calvados
A good spoonful of grained mustard
Some seasoning

## Method

Put the goose fat into a heavy casserole and cook the hocks till the outsides are nicely coloured.
Chop the apples roughly and the garlic finely and add to the casserole.
Cook until the apples are soft and even a bit browned in places, then cover the hocks with cider.
Drink what's left over.
Mix in the mustard and season, put a lid on the casserole and cook in a medium to strong oven for around 90 minutes or until the meat is really tender.
Take the hocks out of the casserole and add the Calvados to the liquid.
Serve with steamed potatoes and about three mange-tout in the French way.

# Chantelle's Pommes Vapeur

The great Chef Careme was said to have devised or collated more than a hundred ways to prepare and cook the humble potato. I am still surprised at how few restaurants seem to offer this simple but delicious alternative to the ubiquitous chip. There can be a little confusion over the name, as *pommes vapeur* can sometimes just mean boiled potatoes. Officially, steamed potatoes are known as *pommes de terre cuites à la vapeur*. Whatever they are officially called, this is how Chantal does them and, for my money, the clever addition of onion and lots of black pepper makes all the difference.

## Ingredients

A kilogram of waxy potatoes
One large onion
Some goose fat
A little salt
Some coarse black pepper

## Method

Peel your potatoes and slice them thinly, not much more than half a centimeter or so.
Peel your onion and slice even more finely than the potatoes.
Put the mixed potatoes and onion in a strong steel colander and dot with some goose fat. (Make sure you use lots of little dots of goose fat and spread them well about, as you will not move the contents of the colander until turning out on to a serving dish).
Sprinkle liberally with salt and freshly grated black pepper.
Put the colander over a large saucepan containing water, cover the colander top with a suitable metal lid, and boil the water.
Steam until potatoes they are on the point of falling apart.

# Néhou

In ancient Norse, the 'hou' part of the name of our village meant 'island' and, apparently, once upon a time, it was.

Nowadays Nehou is joined up with the rest of the area and sits between the start of the *marais* and the lanes and bocaged fields of our old home. The village has an impressive church, a restaurant that in our time closed for lunch, and a museum dedicated to General George Patton.

The leader of the American 'breakout' from the peninsula after D-Day set up his HQ in an orchard just down the road from La Puce, and his granddaughter worked hard to keep his memory and achievements alive. At the end or start of the village and just before the winding road through the *marais* is an impressive church, surrounded by immaculately-maintained gravestones, etched with frequently-recurring names of families who have been born, married and died here for generations.

Across the road is a defiant symbol of a rural France that used to be. Nearly every village would have a bar-grocery store, but few remain. The *bar-epicerie* at Néhou was run by a small but truly formidable woman, and was the headquarters of a daily gathering of local men with an average age of seventy, and I was honoured to be invited to join in. Only partly in irony, I named our group the Jolly Boy's Club. I have never known such a mix of interesting characters, and none more so than the resident immortal:

---

This morning it was our turn for a visit from Dodgy Didier's van. The Bar Ghislaine was packed with those wishing to find a real bargain from the premier Del Boy of the area.

Being an important day, *The Jolly Boys Club was in full attendance. Though having no written constitution or membership regulations, the rules governing full entry to the club are very precise, and include having lived in or on the outskirts of the village since at least birth, having an above average consumption rate of alcohol, and a hard-won understanding of all things to do with the countryside and the nature and true meaning of Life. And, of course, being free to attend at least five meetings every week. Another requirement is to be of an age when one has learned that just waking up each morning is a good start to the day.

I am of course only an associate member, and by far the youngest, especially when compared to our president for life, Old Pierrot. I have not so far been able to discover exactly where he lives or how old he is, but it is casually claimed by the JBC members that he predates the village thanks to his secret elixir of life and special dietary regime, which seems to consist almost entirely of homebrew Calvados. I have also heard it claimed that he has magical powers and was on first-name terms with William the Conqueror.

Whatever the truth about his age and mystic powers, Old Pierrot has become the Merlin to the court of the Jolly Boys Club, and hardly a meeting goes by without him making a mysterious prediction or pronouncement. Last week, he even put a curse on René Ribet for laughing at his yearly forecast of the worst flooding in living memory. It was the talk of the commune when René fell off his moped and broke his wrist on the way home from the meeting. The more superstitious of the villagers credited Old Pierrot's black arts with the accident, but I think it more likely that Mr Johnny Walker was to blame.

*René & Me*

---

*\*It was of course me who came up with the name of the Jolly Boys Club for the informal cabal which met at the Bar Ghislaine. It amused the members, though, being French, they could not see the irony of being called jolly or boys...*

# The Mill of the Flea

I think it must be true that, no matter where we go and how different are the places in which we live, everyone has had a home that they prize above all others.

It might be because they lived there in their formative years and so it represents the treasured memories of the past. It may be where they saw their children grow up, or it may be a place with which, despite all its drawbacks, simply took their hearts.

I worked out recently that we have lived in three countries, five regions of France and a total of 27 homes. Across the Channel, we have lived half-way up a mountain and alongside canals in Brittany, and in a cottage in the shadow of a grandest of châteaux in the Loire Valley. Then there was a brief stay at the manor house on the marshes. But wherever we have been, the Mill of the Flea has never been far from our thoughts and hearts.

It could be that we brought the abandoned mill cottage and farmhouse back to life with our own hands; or that we were young and filled with the boundless enthusiasm and optimism of those years. It could be the memories of all the animals we raised and loved there, or all the small and sometimes farcical adventures in which I became involved. For whatever reason, The Mill of the Flea will always be the home of our hearts in France

Although we have passed this way a dozen times in the decade or more since we drove away from La Puce, we have never been able to bring ourselves to stop. Nor have we visited any old friends, or even the headquarters of the Jolly Boys Club. This is not because I wanted to move on with my life, but because I feared it might be too painful to re-visit the past and be reminded of all that happened here for good and bad. But today, on impulse I brake sharply and turn down the ancient mill track between the copse and the roadside farmhouse.

At the bottom of the track, the *Moulin de la Puce* waits. On the sitting-dog dormer roof sits the terra-cotta pheasant a friend gave us to ensure there would always be food on the table. The original great gable end wall is somehow still standing, overlooking the mill stream and the tiny hump-backed bridge over which wagons laden with sacks of grain bumped for more than two centuries.

We sit in the car for a moment, then decide not to venture into the fields and water meadows behind the cottage where so many memories lie.

Then I back up, turn the car and head up the track for the first time since we said goodbye:

---

Donella is at the big pond saying goodbye to Hen, and before I call her I pick up a rusty nail from the gravel in the turning circle. On the day we arrived at La Puce, I was fascinated by a date and initials scratched by an unknown hand into the stone lintel over the door of the mill cottage. I have often looked at the lintel and wondered about the life and story of whoever made his or her small claim to immortality on that high summer's day in 1776. Now, I take the rusty nail and add our initials and the date.

It is not much of a record, but we have left our mark on La Puce in so many other ways. Because of what we have done here, we know the mill cottage and farmhouse will live on, perhaps even for another two centuries.

My wife arrives beside me and I put my arm across her shoulders. I can see that she has been crying, but she smiles when she sees what I have done before pointing out that I have used the wrong initial for her middle name. I say that it is just about par for the course that I should make one final cock-up before we leave, and we both hug each other and laugh before we cry.

I hand my wife the key to the door, but she shakes her head and goes to wait in the car with Milly the collie. I lock up and look around, I see that we are in for a bumper crop of chestnuts from the tree beside the wooden bridge. Then I remember that it will not be us who will harvest them. Before getting into the car, I look at our old home and hope that it will treat the new owners as kindly as it has treated us across the years, and that they will be as happy here as we have been.

I think it is true to say that home is where the heart is, and wherever our lives take us, a part of our hearts will always rest at La Puce and the Mill of the Flea.

Goodbye old friend, and thanks for all the golden memories.

*French Kisses*

---

A flurry of irritated crows take off from the steeple and the church bell solemnly announces the *midi*.

We have been visiting our old friend the mayor of Néhou. He was the kindest of men and it was my pleasure and privilege that he grazed his cows in our fields. Each year we would accept the rental fee of a dinner at his farmhouse cooked by his lovely wife Solange. The first year the starter was a braised cow's tongue that covered a dinner plate, and there were four more courses.

We walk back to the car and I see that Ghislaine's is open. There are a couple of quite modern cars outside, but unsurprisingly no sign of Mr Janne's tractor or the spectacularly battered Renault that doubled up as old Marcel's runaround and a home for his chickens at night.

My heart stops as I see a familiar-looking moped leaning against the plate glass window by the old metal posters which served as an emergency *pissoir*. (Men were not allowed to use Madame Ghislaine's private facilities).

I walk half-way across the road, and see that the moped is a relatively new model, and not the classic *Mobylette* that was ridden by René Ribet. From the day we arrived at La Puce, René the Fox was my friend and mentor in the ways of the Normandy countryside. His lessons were sometimes expensive, but always worth the cost.

I look at my wife and then at the bar, but she turns her head away. She knows what it going through my mind and does not want to influence my decision.

As I stand in the middle of the road, looking at the past, a figure appears on the grocery store side of the entrance. I see that it is Madame Ghislaine. The years have changed her little, and, as if sensing my presence, she looks out through the window to where we stand.

Our eyes meet but her incurious expression does not alter. She may look the same, but I know that I have changed much since I was a member of the Jolly Boys Club of Néhou. She turns back to her customer, and I turn back to the car.

It has been a fascinating month exploring one of the most beautiful regions of France, and this has been an emotional but fitting climax to our tour.

It has been a revealing and sometimes enchanting month. Wherever we wander in this great and glorious country, Lower Normandy will remain the setting of our first and most passionate love affair with France.

# Local knowledge

This was never meant to be a detailed guide book, but in case you want to look up what we thought of a particular place, here's a list in order of appearance of all the towns visited.

Printed in Great Britain
by Amazon